RIPON CATHEI

Its History and Architecture

by

Bill Forster

Second Edition
edited by Ian Stalker

Includes an Introduction by
the Dean of Ripon

Special drawings: Jen Deadman

Photography and assembly: Ian Stalker

'A cathedral is a good deal more than the sum of its stones'

(Antoine de Saint-Exupéry)

ISBN: 978-0-9531979-0-3

Published by: The Chapter of Ripon Cathedral 2018

c/o Ripon Cathedral Office

Liberty Courthouse, Minster Road

Ripon

North Yorkshire HG4 1QT

United Kingdom

Earlier versions:

First edition: (1993) by Forster, Robson and Deadman.
York: William Sessions Limited (ISBN: 1 850722 119 X)

Second edition: (first imprint 2010) by Forster, Bill.
Ripon: Forster and Stalker (ISBN: 978-0-9531979-0-3)

This second imprint: 2018

All profits from the sale of this book by the Ripon Cathedral Giftshop will benefit the Cathedral

Printed by
The Inter Group, Lingerfield Business Park
Scotton, Knaresborough, North Yorkshire HG5 9JA
Tel: 0800 975 7514

FOREWORD
by the Editor

The first edition of this book was published in 1993. It was the only comprehensive commentary on the history and architecture of Ripon Cathedral since Cecil Hallett's book of 1901. A revised, 2nd Edition appeared in 2010. Now, in 2018, both the above are out of print and a very generous donor, who wishes to remain anonymous, has made this reprint possible.

For this 2018 imprint, changes had to be made to the copyright and publisher details; Dr Bill Forster had passed away in 2014. The installation of a new Dean the same year offered the opportunity for a new introductory statement and update of the appendices. Otherwise, this new imprint is very little changed from the 2nd Edition.

Circumstances did not permit mention in the body text of some physical changes made to the building in the eight years since the first imprint. These are addressed at the end of this foreword.

Bill Forster's book has been widely appreciated by staff and volunteers as well as many Cathedral visitors and students of the Church in England. It proved a good training manual for new Cathedral staff and for volunteer Welcomers and Guides.

Dr Forster amplified and updated the text for the second edition. Happily, Jen Deadman agreed that her wonderful pen drawings could be included. Most of the photographs have been taken more recently.

The sole authorship for the 2nd Edition lay rightly with Bill Forster. He and his late wife, Helen, began a long association with Ripon Cathedral in the nineteen seventies. Many of the views he expresses – often in story form and with humour – are his own, developed during a fifteen-year spell as Dean's Verger and later as voluntary Guide, Welcomer and member of the congregation. His enquiring mind sought answers on the building's past; his open nature encouraged others – clergy, volunteers and visitors – to share their stories and views with him, all to our benefit. This book mostly expresses Bill's personal views, which should not be taken as necessarily those of the Chapter, clergy or staff.

When writing about such an old building it is often difficult to know which of many historical names to allocate to a particular location. Functional areas, such as the Library, Treasury and storage rooms have moved around, and the names of individual chapels have changed many times over the centuries. An appendix addresses this question but, in the text, we have tried to use the current, twenty-first century names to describe locations.

An exception to this is the fairly recent introduction of the spelling **'quire'** to describe the part of the building between the pulpitum screen and the east window, leaving **'choir'** to describe the various singing groups. Making this change throughout the book would have incurred significant printing expense. For economy, we decided that the body text of this imprint would retain the word **'choir'** for both the space and the singers.

Other changes since 2010

The main entrance to the Cathedral has been transformed by the gift in 2012 of glass doors, creating a narthex or vestibule incorporating striking etchings of scenes from the life of St Wilfrid. The effect is to make the Cathedral much more open and welcoming – visitors can look in and see the colour and light of the nave, while those inside can look out to the world the Cathedral serves.

The complete dismantling, cleaning and recalibration of the organ was successfully completed in 2013.

A new feature from 2014 is the wooden Reredos behind the altar in the Chapel of Justice and Peace. It is a reminder of the First World War and the Cathedral's links with Wilfred Owen. It bears words from his poems, based on the theme *"The Pity of War"*.

One other significant but less obvious installation, completed in 2015 – which would certainly have been mentioned by Bill Forster had it happened in his time – is a state-of-the-art CCTV surveillance and security system.

In the wider context of the Diocese, there have been major changes with the creation of the new Anglican Diocese of Leeds which came into being in April 2014. One effect of this was to change the status of the Bishop of Ripon from that of Diocesan Bishop to Area Bishop.

Ian Stalker

CONTENTS

ACKNOWLEDGEMENTS

First Edition (1993)

Bill Forster recorded his thanks to his co-authors, Jen Deadman and Bill Robson and to the many others who made the writing of his book possible. Among those he named were: *Richard Bailey, Paul Barker, Dean Paul Burbridge, Rachel Hellyer, Eric Mansley, Mary Mauchine, and Heinz-Jürgen Ruhl.*

Second Edition, first imprint (2010)

In addition to the above, the joint publishers thanked the following for their invaluable help and advice: *Vicky Crossfield, Gill Brackenbury, Brian Crosse, Sue Ford, Helen Forster, Sheridan Page and David Rivers.*

Second Edition, this imprint (2018)

The following are thanked for their part in modifying the 2010 imprint where necessary and preparing it for reprinting: *Brian Crosse, Sue Ford, Malcolm Hanson, Lynn Shaw, and Ian Stalker.*

As before, these copyright permissions are gratefully acknowledged

- **R.I.B. Library, Reed Book Services**, concerning the quotation from A. de Saint-Exupéry, which first appeared in his *Flight to Arras*, published William Heinemann.

- **Christopher Davies Publishers Ltd**, concerning John Ormond's poem, *Cathedral Builders*.

- **The Chapter of Ripon Cathedral**, concerning material from *The Architecture of Ripon Cathedral* (L. Harrison and J. Deadman, William Sessions, 1980) and *Ripon Cathedral Stained Glass: the Complete Record* (D. Balmforth, Maxiprint, 1991).

- **SPCK**, concerning quotations from *History of the People of England* (A. D. Greenwood, SPCK, 1921).

- **B.T.Batsford Ltd**, concerning quotations from *The Greater English Church in the Middle Ages* by Harry Batsford and Charles Fry (London B. T. Batsford Ltd, 1940).

INTRODUCTION

by the Very Revd John Dobson, the Dean of Ripon

The cathedrals of England have been enjoying something of a renaissance in the first decades of the twenty-first century. There is a greater appreciation of their historical and architectural significance, genuine delight in the beauty of their fabric, liturgy and music, and an acceptance of their valuable contribution to culture, the arts and social cohesion. This has all found expression in increased numbers of worshippers, pilgrims and visitors. Most of these people who venture to cross a cathedral's threshold wish to learn more about its history and architecture. Ripon Cathedral is no exception in enjoying the benefits of this welcome phenomenon, and its visitors are no different in their desire to learn more. This second imprint of the second edition of Bill Forster's much-enjoyed *Ripon Cathedral, its history and architecture* enriches a visit and provides continued enjoyment over prolonged reflection.

One of the first pastoral visits that I made after arriving in Ripon as Dean in 2014 was to Bill Forster in Harrogate Hospital. Just days before his sad death, I was fortunate to find him at a lucid moment. His passion for Ripon Cathedral was clear. That resonated with me, myself having known and loved this building since my childhood. What I was later to discover by reading the second edition of this book, was that Bill Forster's passion had been matched by an almost encyclopaedic knowledge of the development of this remarkable building. It confirmed what I already knew, I still had more to discover about this wonderful place.

Bill's love for Ripon Cathedral, matched by that of the group of people who worked with him and Ian Stalker to produce his book, is quite understandable when one pauses to take in the remarkable nature of its long, rich history and varied architecture. The numinous Anglo-Saxon crypt, dedicated by St. Wilfrid in 672AD, represents the oldest built-fabric of all English cathedrals. Symbolising the empty tomb of the risen Christ it has borne witness to the foundation of the Christian faith for over thirteen hundred years. The captivatingly varied architectural styles above ground tell a story of the development of the church's life not only on this site but throughout these islands and across Europe. They have much to teach about the merits of combining steadfast faithfulness with a willingness to adapt and embrace new possibilities.

Full of life in the twenty-first century, Ripon Cathedral seeks to serve its city and diocese by doing just that. The stunning narthex completed in 2012 shows how contemporary architects can complement the achievements of their forebears. The doors speak of a spirituality and culture of generous hospitality and welcome. The decoration on the glass panels tell the story of St. Wilfrid, our founding missionary bishop, whose desire to share his faith in Christ and serve the people inspires us still. The impact of this is seen in how many are drawn in to worship enlivened by a rich diet of choral music, itself tracing its association with Ripon back to the seventh-century; and in the use of this building as a hub for concerts, art festivals, and large public meetings that benefit people from across the region and beyond.

In his introduction to the Second Edition in 2010, my predecessor, the late Keith Jukes, wrote in reference to its reader who visits Ripon Cathedral, "What you will find will further bring the pages of this book to life and, by coming, you will be joining with the countless people who have journeyed to Ripon down the centuries and found something unique and worthwhile for their mind and their soul." This still remains the case with this second impression.

May God richly bless you.   John R. Dobson, Trinity Sunday 2018

Etched glass panel from the 2012 narthex:
St Wilfrid returning to Ripon from one of his visits to Rome

Part 1: Chapters 1 to 8

History

from c.650 to today

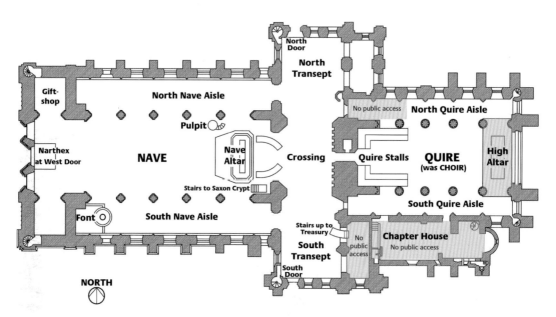

The main areas of the Cathedral at ground level

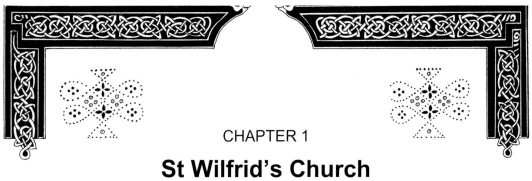

CHAPTER 1

St Wilfrid's Church
(c.650 - 950)

RIPON'S EARLY HISTORY can be summed up in the one word – **Wilfrid**: abbot, bishop, missionary and traveller.

In life his personality dominated the church in Northumbria, whilst in death the veneration of his remains brought wealth and fame to the church that he had founded in Ripon.

The town's origins had been anything but peaceful. Sometime early in the sixth century Anglian invaders swept over the North Sea and settled on the Yorkshire coast. Some penetrated westwards up the River Ure and where the Skell branches off they founded Ripon, naming it after their tribe - like Repton in Derbyshire. Their fighting days over, they settled to a pastoral life of growing crops, catching fish and rearing animals.

Under the influence of the pagan invaders much of England abandoned the Christian faith although, in the sixth century, Columba had established at Iona off the west coast of Scotland, a vibrant community which made significant progress in establishing Christianity in parts of Scotland and later, Northumbria. Meanwhile the Pope sent first Augustine, then Paulinus to re-establish the faith in England. Paulinus worked successfully for many years in Kent then went to Northumbria, taking with him Ethelburga (the Christian daughter of the Kentish king) whose marriage had been arranged to Edwin, the pagan king of Northumbria.

Soon after the marriage, Edwin called a meeting of his chiefs to consider whether Paulinus should be allowed to preach the new religion. The scholar Bede recorded the proceedings, which included one of the finest passages in early English literature. It describes how one of Edwin's chiefs sought to compare the brief, earthly life of man with the time of which they lacked knowledge. 'It was like a sparrow', he said, 'flying on a winter's night into a king's hall, where all was light and warmth, safe from winter storms. After passing briefly through the hall, it leaves by another door, back into the darkness'. Man likewise, he argued, is seen briefly then departs. 'If', he went on, 'the new religion will reveal to us new knowledge, it is right that we should follow it'.

Edwin accepted the Christian faith forthwith and was baptised at a small, newly built wooden church in York. The future of the new religion seemed assured, many people were baptised by Paulinus and another church was built, this time at Catterick. Paulinus' success was however short-lived, because Edwin's army was routed by an army from Mercia. Edwin was killed and Paulinus fled south. As the Venerable Bede wrote later, 'there was dreadful slaughter among the Northumbrian church and nation'.

During Edwin's reign, Oswald, the son of Edwin's predecessor, had taken refuge with the monks of Iona and on succeeding Edwin as king, he appealed to those monks for help in restoring Christianity to his kingdom. As a result, Aidan was sent from Iona to found a monastery on the island of Lindisfarne, within sight of the royal palace at Bamburgh. It was a crucial step in the permanent establishment of the church in Northumbria.

Under Aidan and his successors, monasteries were built at Jarrow, Wearmouth, Hartlepool, Whitby and Ripon. Excavations at Jarrow and Wearmouth in recent years by Professor Rosemary Cramp have greatly increased our knowledge of the period, and the story is depicted in a notable exhibition at Jarrow Hall, alongside the church. Ripon's first monastery was established by the Lindisfarne monks a few years after Aidan's death, in the middle of the seventh century. The site was probably close to 'Priest-ley' (the open place of the priests), a short distance north east of the present cathedral and now called Priest Lane. Some very old carved stones have been found in the area, but the monastery may very well have been built in wood.

Not long after the establishment of the monastery, Wilfrid arrived in Ripon. A Northumbrian by birth, he had enjoyed the patronage of the Queen, trained at Lindisfarne, then stayed in Rome absorbing the splendour of worship there. He no doubt made a mental note of customs in the Celtic church at home (and derived successively from Iona and Lindisfarne) and found them out of step with practices of the modern Roman Church .

Disagreement was inevitable when he returned to Ripon. The King supported Wilfrid in favouring Roman ways, so the Celtic-trained monks returned north. Wilfrid founded a monastery, probably just north or north-west of the present cathedral, and he became abbot. Under his leadership, Ripon was possibly the first English abbey to adopt the Benedictine rule. The King endowed it with either 30 or 40 hides of land (a hide was about 90 acres), which led a 19th-century writer to suggest that Ripon contained 30 or 40 thatched dwellings in Wilfrid's day.

The year 664 was a turning point for the church in England. Confusion was widespread throughout Northumbria because some Christians followed Celtic customs, and others Roman. Matters came to a head when the King was celebrating Easter whilst his wife was still fasting in preparation for it!

A synod was called at Hilda's abbey of Whitby and Wilfrid was instrumental in persuading the Celtic church to adopt Roman procedures in future. This ensured that the English church was in step with the church on the continent, a unity that lasted for nearly nine centuries.

Another development at about that time was the establishment of a school in Ripon. Bishop Moorman related that, after Benedict Biscop had returned to England in 669, there were schools at Canterbury, York and Ripon.

Wilfrid exercised a crucial role in modifying the course of the church whilst Biscop, who had also trained at Lindisfarne and Rome, introduced a totally new technique into northern England, that of building in stone. Some while before his day, a Saxon poet had marvelled at the stone arches and massive stone walls which he had seen in a deserted Roman city. In the poet's day, even royal palaces (like Yeavering and Cheddar) were built of wood and it is hard to imagine the sensation that building in stone must have created.

Wilfrid's biographer records that the new church at Ripon was dedicated to St Peter on the saint's day in 672. Nearby, another church – the Ladykirk – was probably built about the same time; it was described by the historian Leland in the 16th century. Wilfrid's foundation was clearly of considerable size and importance because it is known that the King and his court stayed there for a while later in its history.

Who was actually bishop of (or at) Ripon? Perhaps the answer is as follows: first it was Wilfrid himself, as bishop of part of Northumbria with his seat at Ripon. Next followed Eadhed, who Bede says was Bishop of Ripon from 681-686. Finally, in later life, Wilfrid became bishop at Ripon once more. The story is complex, and experts differ over details, but it serves to explain the unusual position that Ripon held in the northern church for so long, being at times virtually another cathedral within a larger diocese.

It is of interest that Ripon had a link with Jarrow, inasmuch as Jarrow's first abbot was Ceolfrid, the former baker at Wilfrid's monastery. At Jarrow the scholar Bede made great use of the library founded by Biscop and won posthumous renown as 'the father of English historians'. As historian, theologian, scientist and poet, he stands as one of the great scholars of all time.

Wilfrid's life story, perhaps the first ever of an Englishman, was written by 'Stephen of Ripon'. He is often referred to as 'Eddius Stephanus', and it is not totally clear if the two Stephens are the same person. The work is full of interest but, whereas Bede was noted for his impartiality, it has been said of this biographer that whenever he depicted Wilfrid in controversy, Wilfrid was in the right and his enemies in the wrong! Eddius was one of Wilfrid's monks so, if he was the writer, the bias is not surprising.

Certainly Wilfrid had a clear vision of what the church should do and how it should achieve it. His determination and his frequent disagreements with the authorities of both church and state brought him enemies, but Northumbria was a pagan land and it needed Wilfrid's drive as well as Aidan's simplicity and Cuthbert's saintliness to secure the firm establishment of the church.

In his lifetime Wilfrid travelled vast distances. He did much missionary work on the south coast of England, went three times to Rome and was for a while a missionary in Friesland, although not a very successful one. Subsequently, however, one of his monks – Willibrord – preached the Gospel to the Friesians then went on to Luxembourg. Willibrord's body rests today in the church at Echternach, at which on Whit Tuesday each year, there are the kind of festivities so familiar to Ripon people in the middle ages ... 'a mingling of the devout, the jovial and the grotesque', as one writer has put it.

Late in the eighth century there were ... 'terrible portents that miserably affected the inhabitants of Northumbria', with 'dreadful lightning and dragons flying in the air'. Soon afterwards, much of the kingdom suffered plunder and slaughter at the hands of the Vikings, but it was not until the middle of the next century that Ripon too, suffered. A former historical panel in the cathedral said that the Danes destroyed St Wilfrid's church and the notion probably stems from a book written in 1808. Scholars today doubt whether such destruction occurred, and it cannot be reconciled with the evidence of Eadmer and the Anglo-Saxon Chronicle (see later in this chapter).

By the early 10th century, Athelstan (grandson of Alfred and the first king of all England) had achieved peace with the Danes who then occupied much of England. He visited Ripon and Beverley in 926 and 937 and at each place established 'Liberties', as at Hexham. This was part of a policy aimed at stabilising the northern boundary of his kingdom. The perimeter of the Liberty of St Wilfrid was marked by eight boundary crosses of which one stump still stands in nearby Sharow. Until a century ago there was another near present day Kangel (Archangel) Close.

Within the Liberty, sanctuary was assured for all fugitives, whether murderers, thieves or debtors. It may seem strange that the church protected such people, but one of Athelstan's motives was to end blood feuds. Heavy penalties – even death – faced those who failed to respect the sanctuary guaranteed by his charter.

Face incorporated in corbel table. N.W. tower

The fugitives were called *grythmen* or *gyrthmen* (*gryth* meant peace); a *gryth priest* was responsible for their welfare and the ultimate place of refuge was the gryth stool inside the church: those at Hexham and Beverley still survive.

Athelstan's charter was a major factor behind the power of the church in the centuries that followed, but within a few decades Ripon suffered heavily for belonging to the Viking kingdom of York, ruled by Eric Bloodaxe. Its street names today testify to that period: Skellgate, Blossomgate and so on, where 'gate' is the Scandinavian for 'way'. The English King, Eadred, brought his forces north to assert his authority over the rebel kingdom and in the action that followed he devastated the area around the minster, destroying by fire both St Wilfrid's church and monastery. Many thousands of Northumbrians died and as Eadmer wrote later, the ruined church at Ripon became the home 'not of priests but of wild beasts'. The Anglo-Saxon Chronicle gives the date of destruction as 950.

To the monks of the time it was catastrophic. They could never have guessed that similar disasters would strike again in the 11th century (the harrying of the north) and in the 14th (the Scots raids). Nor could they know that after each disaster, the church would rise to yet greater splendour – but that is anticipating future chapters.

Adapted from a painting by David Mayo, 2010

Impression of St Wilfrid's crypt in its early days; the main structure of this first sanctuary is little changed since it was built around 672. At some stage, steps were built below the 'eye of the needle' aperture, back left.

The walls were plastered and painted in recent times.

CHAPTER 2

What followed St Wilfrid's church?

(c.950-1180)

WHAT HAPPENED TO ST WILFRID'S BODY after 950? Compared with the destruction of his church, this might seem a trivial matter but the truth is otherwise. In the medieval church relics were the supreme status symbol and their magnetism assured both the liberality of pilgrims and the bounty of the deceased. It was an area in which fraud became regrettably common as more than one church claimed to have possession of the same relic.

When both Canterbury and Ripon claimed to have the remains of Wilfrid of Ripon, who was right?

Eadmer, in his *Life of St Wilfrid* described how, around 952, Archbishop Odo came to Ripon to see St Wilfrid's devastated church. On the appointed day he was joined by two men who were staying locally and they opened up the ground where St Wilfrid (of Ripon) lay. They gave the bones and dust to Odo 'to take to Canterbury', retaining all but a part which was put 'in a convenient place'.

The noted 19th-century historian, Professor Willis, published a ground plan of the Roman and Saxon Cathedral of Canterbury, showing that the remains of St Wilfrid of Ripon were interred beneath the altar situated in the most sacred spot of the church, the eastern apse.

But had Odo taken the right Wilfrid? We turn to Eadmer again, this time his *Life of St Oswald, Archbishop of York 979-992*. After a night's vigil of prayer, Oswald and his men dug up the pavement of the ruined church at Ripon and found, with several bodies, a tablet saying 'Here lie St Wilfrid bishop of York' (and five named abbots). Eadmer adds that a shrine was made for this Wilfrid – Wilfrid II – 'who was joined by blood to the great Wilfrid and who succeeded him in rule over the church of York'. Eadmer's writings leave little doubt that the great medieval shrine at Ripon contained the remains not of Wilfrid of Ripon, but of his successor bishop at York, Wilfrid II. But Eadmer aside, is it likely that Odo, seeking so great a prize, would return with the wrong one?

From confusion, we can pass to certainty. In the ninth century, the monks of Lindisfarne had retreated south in the face of Viking invasion, taking with them the body of St Cuthbert. After settling for a century at Chester-le-Street, fresh troubles caused them to move to Ripon, where a new shrine to St Wilfrid had been completed just three years previously. The arrival of St Cuthbert's body must have aroused a great sense of poignancy and thanksgiving, for Cuthbert had been a monk at the first monastery in Ripon. He left when Wilfrid became abbot, to become himself first abbot, and later bishop, of Lindisfarne. Cuthbert's body rested here for only a short while then the monks took his coffin to a hastily built church at Durham, to which the see of Bernicia (northern Northumbria) had just been transferred. It was only centuries later, that the coffin was found to contain not only Cuthbert's remains, but the head of St Aidan and such priceless objects as Cuthbert's pectoral cross and the Lindisfarne gospels.

Little is known of Ripon church in 995 but its very fitness to house St Cuthbert's remains must be a measure of its renown. From around that time the Archbishops of York resided in Ripon and, as will become evident, they and the canons of Ripon minster became all-powerful in the affairs of the town.

After the northern part of Eadred's kingdom had been punished for its Viking sympathies – whether spontaneous or enforced – it enjoyed barely a century of recovery before the Norman Conquest.

Meanwhile the church made changes. Prayers had to be said for the King at each service as a means of instilling loyalty into his subjects. He was not merely head of the church but *Vicar of Christ among a Christian folk*. Paganism was a more serious problem, entailing the passing of laws that forbade the veneration of trees or stones as holy places. The veneration of wells had been recorded by Bede with enthusiasm, but clearly the boundary between the sacred and the profane was beginning to cause concern.

The doctrine of the Immaculate Conception and devotion to the Blessed Virgin Mary became increasingly a feature of worship in English churches, although no less a man than Bernard of Clairvaux had attacked the idea that she was different from other humans. Indeed, some continental theologians dismissed the movement as *an aberration from the foggy isle*. Today's feminist movement seeks, among other things, to give a higher dignity to women. Perhaps that was also in the minds of those long-gone theologians?

Moorman notes that, in the 10th century, priests often married, especially in the north. Another writer has commented that this was true for two centuries after the Norman Conquest. So the church's conversion from Celtic ways to Roman ideals, which St Wilfrid had ostensibly achieved at the Synod of Whitby, had still some way to go!

Ripon is first recorded as being a collegiate church in the days of Aldred of York (1060-1069) and the earliest named canons date from around 1140. The shorthand for *collegiate church of canons* is simply *minster* which derives from the same Latin word as *monastery*. Whereas, however, the priests of a monastery spent their time mostly within the building, those of a minster served the spiritual needs of the district around them. At Ripon, this district extended as far west as Nidderdale, some 10 miles away.

The minster enjoyed considerable prestige: a 10th-century book mentions a bishop's seat at Ripon and another record, compiled between 1094 and 1109, says that York had five bishoprics which included Ripon, Beverley and Whitby, all places of importance in St Wilfrid's day.

Just as the northerners had to be brought to heel in the days of the Viking kingdom of Yorvik, so they rebelled – more than once – against the rule of William I after 1066 and 'it took two months to slaughter and burn from Ouse to Tees as William wished' (Greenwood). Whether the minster suffered at this time is not known with certainty. The *Domesday Book* of 1086 recorded that in Ripon there were eight villeins and ten husbandmen with six ploughs. From both Domesday and earlier records a clear picture emerges of the pattern of settlement in the area, one that has changed little, apart from the expansion of Ripon itself, up to modern times. Some places recorded then cannot be identified or have since been deserted, others are actually smaller now than then. Even the spelling of names has not greatly changed, e.g. Mercinga-ton/Markington; Stodlege/Studley; Gythinga Deal/Givendale and so on which adds to the feeling one has in Ripon, of continuity with the past.

The Domesday survey is the one event associated by most people with the reign of William I but the church courts introduced by the first great Norman archbishops survived for hundreds of years. Clerics tried in them tended to face lighter penalties than if they had faced a civil court, but the courts also tried lay people on moral lapses, matters concerning marriage and quarrels over wills. We shall meet examples in chapter four.

By the early 12th century, at least two hospitals had been founded in Ripon. St John's, immediately south of the Skell was the earlier, the present chapel dating only from the nineteenth century. St Mary's was built a few years later in what is now Magdalen's Road but was then the main route north out of Ripon. Each hospital had its own priest, provided accommodation for poor people and was obliged to give travelling lepers food and drink for the night: leprosy was an unpleasant consequence of the crusades from the 11th century onwards.

To local people today St Mary's is still *The leper chapel*. It was splendidly restored a few years ago and is used regularly for worship.

The borough of Ripon was established around the middle of the 12th century. Henry I granted a charter for a four days fair, then soon afterwards Stephen granted further privileges and also confirmed earlier ones from the days of Edward the Confessor and William the Conqueror.

A certain event in Henry I's reign would have aroused little concern among Ripon's citizens. A band of monks from St Mary's at York arrived here one Christmas-tide. After celebrating mass at the minster they departed up the valley of the Skell, intent upon founding their own monastery. For two years they were almost destitute but in 1134 were given the resources to start building Fountains Abbey. Their great Cistercian foundation, with its huge flocks of sheep, laid the foundations of Ripon's highly prosperous cloth trade in the centuries ahead. Riponians of 1132 could little have guessed the significance of that Christmas arrival.

A few years later, local people suffered in the turbulence which marked the war between King Stephen and his cousin the Empress Matilda, who was described by an admiring chronicler as 'having nothing of a woman about her but all the courage of a knight'. Her uncle, King David of Scotland, invaded England in her support and at Northallerton in 1138 the Archbishop of York arranged the standards of the three great churches – York, Ripon and Beverley – on a cart, to inspire the English. Military history was made, as the decisive victory over the Scots was the first ever in England by archers and foot soldiers (the Battle of the Standard).

Two years later trouble spread to Ripon itself. Around 1140 Alan, Earl of Richmond, had fortified 'Hutton', which was almost certainly Hutton Conyers, about two miles north east of the town. The castle site is marked today only by irregular mounds and is shown on the current 1: 25,000 edition Ordnance Survey map. Using that base, the earl burst into St Wilfrid's church and attacked the archbishop himself at St Wilfrid's shrine. In his day, the earl was reviled by Ripon people because he refused to sell corn from his own store at a time of famine.

It is of interest that some 30 years later the new Archbishop of York was Roger de Pont l'Evêque. In earlier days he had been a companion of Thomas à Becket, but took the King's side in the final quarrel between them and so came to be regarded as an accessory to Becket's murder in Canterbury Cathedral.

Not long after Beckett's death, Archbishop Roger initiated work on the magnificent new church at Ripon, of which so much still stands. Knowing Roger's tainted reputation and taking account of the dread in which Christians at that time viewed the terrors of hell, could it be that today's Ripon Cathedral is directly linked to the murder of Thomas à Becket? Was its building a supreme act of expiation by Archbishop Roger?

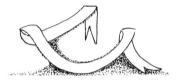

CHAPTER 3

The period of

Archbishops Roger and de Grey

(c.1180-1260)

THE LATE NORMAN CHURCH OF WHICH MUCH STANDS TODAY was initiated by Archbishop Roger (c.1174) and modified and completed by Archbishop Walter de Grey (c.1260). Together they set it upon its *grand period of growth*. Many embellishments were added in the centuries that followed but the only significant structural additions were the Lady Chapel in the 14th, and the nave aisles in the 16th century.

From that far-off period, it is interesting to identify beliefs and practices that were to merge, three centuries hence, in the chaos of *reformation*.

Had Riponians of the day been told about Magna Carta, it is unlikely that they would have shown any interest. Still less would they have been concerned by the fact that a few years earlier, the University of Paris gave its consent to the teaching of Aristotle's ideas. Aristotle, the father of modern science, emphasised the importance of observation, a viewpoint that was anathema to the Church with its dogmatic hold over men's minds. The consequences, not just for the church at Ripon but for most of Europe, would be eventually devastating.

Danger for the church of a different kind lay in its exploitation of relics – as early as 1179 it was ruled that priests were neither to sell nor show them for money. And in the same year as Magna Carta (1215), the Lateran Council had to set rules restricting the veneration of objects. How could historians of the day have foreseen the consequences?

Of more immediate concern to Ripon people than these changes was their denial of the chalice at the Eucharist. In future, they were to receive only the bread.

On the material side, the townspeople were already benefiting from their new neighbours, the Cistercian monks at Fountains Abbey. With estates that spread eventually over 151 parishes and as far west as the Lake District, their great flocks of sheep provided raw material for the prosperous trade in woollen cloth that developed in Ripon and many other Yorkshire towns. From 20 July 1394 to 4 November 1395, we know the cloth output of several Yorkshire towns:

> *Pontefract, Howden, Selby 203 cloths*
>
> *Wakefield, Leeds, Doncaster 254 cloths*
>
> *Richmond, Bedale, Northallerton 332 cloths*
>
> *Ripon, Boroughbridge 431 cloths*

The town's earliest surviving record relates to an Exchequer grant for repairing the fuller's house at Ripon; that was in 1186. Fulling was the process of *filling* out the cloth by trampling it in human dung and urine, then *walking* it in water to cleanse it. Some years later, two charters of Fountains Abbey were witnessed by several of the gentry and by William the Dyer of Ripon, who was clearly a man of importance in the town.

Quite early in the history of Fountains Abbey (founded in 1134), a formal agreement had been reached between the abbey and the canons of Ripon that neither would take lands or income without the other's consent. Perhaps there had been trouble before that, but this definition of *spheres of influence* ensured harmonious relations for the rest of the Middle Ages.

Archbishop de Grey's name is associated today with the west front which he added to Roger's nave and which is now accepted as one of the finest examples of this new Early English style of building in England.

But he was not popular with the Minster. By virtue of Athelstan's charter, the canons claimed authority over the whole Liberty, which would have included some of the land of the Archbishop's palace. This, in 1228, de Grey disputed and in collusion with the King's sheriff he deliberately created a breach of the peace.

The canons thereupon summoned both the Archbishop's bailiff and the sheriff to appear before their own court with the King's justices present. To the gratification of later historians the proceedings were recorded in great detail, enough in fact to give us a fairly good idea of the town plan at the time. The canons' powers are set out in detail and will be mentioned in later chapters. The mere fact that they, like the Archbishop, owned about one half of the town indicates the extent of their hold over it.

Judgement was found against the bailiff and the sheriff and heavy fines were imposed. It is of interest that a century earlier, the sheriff had invaded the Liberty of St Wilfrid, but on that occasion the Archbishop supported the canons and the invaders withdrew. The 1228 case seems to have established the authority of the canons irrefutably and no such incident occurred again!

We noted the confusion surrounding the remains of Wilfrid I and Wilfrid II. It was de Grey who took the first steps towards building the legendary cult of St Wilfrid for which Ripon was so famous in the closing centuries of the Middle Ages. He had Wilfrid's remains transferred to a different part of the church, but the head was kept separate from the body, as was common practice in those days.

CHAPTER 4

From riches to privation
(1260-1547)

INTRODUCTION

Although this chapter covers nearly three centuries, the town's population rose but little. The exact figure for 1260 is not known but a century later it has been estimated at 1,250 and three centuries further on again, had only risen by an additional one-third.

During the period, the prosperity of both the Church and of Ripon's trade in woollen cloth had increased substantially, only to plummet as the Reformation drew near.

By the early 14th century the production of cloth was the town's principal occupation and in time Ripon and Boroughbridge together made more cloth than any Yorkshire town, save York. Then in 1460, Halifax's output exceeded Ripon's and the town's pre-eminence was over. After visiting Ripon early in the 16th century, the historian Leland wrote ... 'there were on the far bank of the Skell a great number of tainters (stretchers) for woollen cloth to be made, but now idleness is sore increased in the town and cloth making almost decayed'.

In 1295, Ripon had sent two MP's to the Model Parliament, reflecting the town's prosperity and importance. This was repeated a few times in the succeeding century, then from 1553 it became a regular occurrence. In modern times, the constituency has been merged with that of Skipton. The main military feature of the period (1260-1546) was the ruinous Scots' raids of the early 14th century. By 1314, the monks of Fountains Abbey had had to flee to Bedale, where they took refuge in the church tower. Four years later, the Lanercost Chronicle records that the Scots burned the nearby towns of Northallerton and Boroughbridge then pushed on to Ripon ... 'where they despoiled the town of all the goods they could find'. Then ... 'from those who entered the mother church and defended it against the Scottish army they exacted 1000 marks instead of burning the town itself'.

The Archbishop of York addressed the Dean and Chapter of St Peter's York on the subject, referring to … 'nefarious crimes, horrid deeds and hostile savagery' and to … 'disturbing the peace of the Liberty of Ripon': an earlier chapter has mentioned how seriously the Minster regarded that offence. The Archbishop ordered excommunication to be pronounced … 'on all who perpetrate deeds of this kind'. He instructed his bailiff to collect from the people of Ripon the fine demanded by the Scots, 'having considered the ability of the people to pay – since you have better knowledge of the condition of the people'. Two years later in fact the fine was still unpaid and hostages were still in prison.

Next year (1319), the Scots again threatened the countryside and this time the Archbishop rallied the people of York together with priests and clerks to face the Scots at Myton-on-Swale, not far from Boroughbridge. It was a catastrophic move, for in the action that followed the Scots slaughtered great numbers and forced hordes into the Swale, where they drowned. In a letter to the Pope, the Archbishop wrote of … 'my manor of Ripon latterly destroyed by the Scots'.

Still more misery followed for at the end of that year, disease broke out on a great scale among the oxen and cows so that …'few animals of any kind were left … … and men had to plough with horses'.

The Scots threatened again a few years later and the Archbishop ordered John de Clotherum to 'array men of Ripon able and sufficient to carry arms so that they are sufficiently armed to set out with him'.

As the Scots threat receded it was followed by first the Hundred Years War with France, and then the Wars of the Roses. There is no firm evidence that ordinary townsfolk were involved to any great extent in either, save that medieval wills of the period (even of clergymen) often feature swords, battleaxes and the like. Nearby Wensleydale was a recruiting ground for Salisbury in 1458 in the Wars of the Roses, then was over-run in the following year by the Percys (who had allied with Margaret of Anjou), but Ripon escaped the turmoil.

In the 16th century, affairs in the Church began to reflect the turmoil in the land and the Middle Ages were fast drawing to a close.

14th century misericord

In 1535, acting on information supplied by his very efficient civil servant, Thomas Cromwell, Henry VIII secured the dissolution of all the smaller monasteries. This caused ordinary people to fear that Henry's next move would be an assault on the treasures of parish churches and they reacted sharply. One consequence was the ill-fated Pilgrimage of Grace which led among other things to the beheading of the former Abbot of Fountains. A few years later, Fountains Abbey was dissolved and by the end of our chapter, Ripon Minster had no canons, few of its medieval treasures and a very small income. The Reformation had arrived and the church *in* England was poised to become the Church *of* England.

TOWN AND TOWNSFOLK

This book is about the story of the Minster and its architecture. Of what relevance is a section on the town and its occupants?

In today's secular Britain, it is hard to realise the interdependence that existed in the Middle Ages between church and townsfolk. The people needed the means of escaping eternal damnation which the church offered (or sold), whilst the church needed for its survival the indemnities and gifts of the faithful.

Before considering the various ways in which Church and people interacted, it will be helpful to find out what sort of town medieval Ripon was, and what sort of lives the inhabitants led.

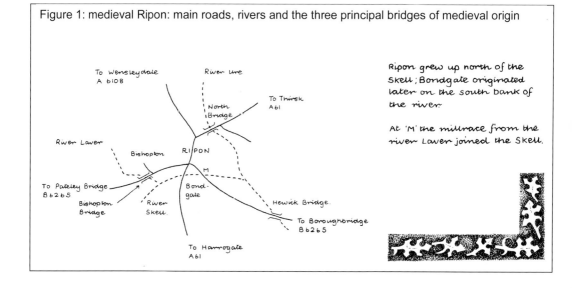

Figure 1: medieval Ripon: main roads, rivers and the three principal bridges of medieval origin

THE TOWN

Ripon's survival in early days was bound up with its rivers (see Figure 1). The Skell in particular provided water for drinking, brewing, thatching, plastering and no doubt waste disposal. In addition, as early as the Norman Conquest, a mill race ran from the Laver (starting below Bishopton Bridge) and joined the Skell near point 'M'. From about 1200, it provided power for the Archbishop's corn mill and the water needed for fulling cloth.

As the Middle Ages advanced, Ripon merchants began to export cloth across the North Sea. They needed access to ports like Hull and the bridges over the Ure were essential for trade: both North Bridge and Hewick Bridge date back at least as far as the early 13th century.

In early times the routes westwards simply followed the Rivers Laver and Skell and Bishopton Bridge is probably later in origin than the Ure bridges. In the town itself the Skell was crossed by at least two bridges but their exact locations are uncertain.

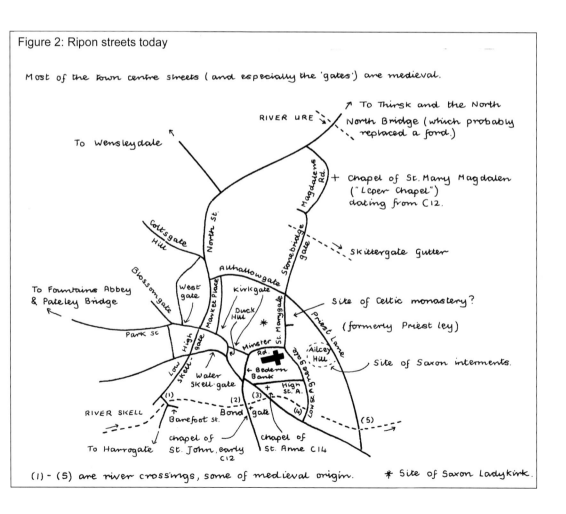

Figure 2: Ripon streets today

Most of the town centre streets (and especially the 'gates') are medieval.

To Thirsk and the North

RIVER URE

North Bridge (which probably replaced a ford.)

To Wensleydale

+ Chapel of St. Mary Magdalen ("Leper Chapel") dating from C12.

Skittergate Gutter

Coltsgate Hill

North St.

Blossomgate

Stonebridgegate

Allhallowgate

To Fountains Abbey & Pateley Bridge

West gate

Kirkgate

Site of Celtic monastery?

(formerly Priest ley)

Duck Hill

Park St

High gate

Minster Rd.

St. Marygate

Priest Lane

Ailcey Hill

Site of Saxon interments.

Low Skellgate

Market Place

Water Skellgate

Bedern Bank

High St. A.

RIVER SKELL

Barefoot St.

Bondgate

Low St. A.

(1)   (2)   (3)   (4)   (5)

To Harrogate

chapel of St. John, early C12

chapel of St. Anne C14

(1) - (5) are river crossings, some of medieval origin.   * Site of Saxon Ladykirk.

For supplies of drinking water, a fortunate minority had access to St Wilfrid's well which was located within the churchyard. From time to time new hemp cords were needed for it, also a bucket bound with iron, two *trendelys* and a *magnum puly*. In 1425 Edmund Loksmith supplied a key for the gate and another was required in the following year. Use of the well was probably restricted to the staff of the minster. Figure 2 shows the pattern of the town's streets today, one which has changed little over the centuries. The majority of streets then, as now, were named *gates*, the Viking word for *way*. Priest Ley *(field)* was exceptional and describes the open space of the Celtic monks nearby. The main route north from that site was over the Skittergate Gutter, past the Norman chapel and on to the river. *Skitter* describes an unfortunate human affliction.

The Archbishop's palace stood to the north of Kirkgate: one entrance was under the archway seen today on the north side of the street, near the east end. The palace was second only in importance to the minster. Since Saxon times there had been a Ladykirk just north of the minster and in time, the town gained three hospitals. Only ruins survive of the chapel to St Anne's hospital but that of St Mary Magdalen is an elegant Norman building, used regularly for worship.

In 1304, Nicholas of Bondgate gave land to the minster for the building of a Bedern, or house of prayer, in which the vicars of the church would live; it was probably to the west of Bedern Bank. A new Bedern was built about a century later on the site now occupied by the Old Deanery Restaurant in Minster Road.

A thought for your pennies...

Not every reader will be familiar with the old, non-decimal currency used in Britain up to February, 1971.

The 'new penny' introduced in that year was worth 2.4 'old pennies', as there had been 240 'old pennies' to the pound. The paper pound sterling (£) note was the only monetary unit retained for long after decimalisation, although it was replaced by the £ coin twelve years later.

Prior to 1971, a pound was worth 240 pence or 20 shillings (i.e. 12 pence to the shilling). A sum of money was expressed by spelling out the number of full pounds (£), shillings (s) and pence (p) involved, e.g. £4 12s 6d, which would translate as £4.625 in the new decimal system. How? Well......

12s 6d = (12x12) + 6 = 150 'old pennies' = 150/2.4 = 62.5 'new pence'.

A reconstruction of the Maison de Dieu, or Hospital of St. Anne, as drawn by the Reverend Lukis, 1872. The ruin of the chapel remains; the hospital was destroyed in 1869.

The bakehouse appears in old records and in the 14th century there were four shops in Kirkgate. The number elsewhere in the town is not known but each was perhaps little more than a room with a shelf outside for displaying their wares, reminiscent of surviving old shops in York's Shambles.

A few of the houses in town had substantial roofs of stone slate but for the majority, thatch had to suffice. Barley straw was used for cheaper jobs, but rye (about 2.5 times as dear) for better quality work. Women often had the tedious task of wetting and straightening the straw for the thatchers.

Most people who lived all their lives in the same house could expect it to be substantially rebuilt at some time, with new roof timbers and thatch, repairs to the wattle and daub between the wall timbers, the mending of doors and window shutters and the renewal of clay floors. The minster was the only building in town to have glass in its windows.

All property was owned by either the archbishop or the canons, to whom rents were payable. If we take full account of incomes and prices, then and now, we find that housing – which was of poor quality – was cheap, beer was cheap, but food was much dearer. People had few possessions and even in homes that could afford to have a written will prepared, it was normal to specify the recipients for a cloak, a shirt, bedspread, 'best spoon' and kitchen utensils. The usual fuel was wood, but one will mentions: 'all my coal'. Unusual bequests included a unicorn (any connection with the Unicorn Hotel in town?) and a belt designed to hold ingredients used as charms.

How did Ripon people earn their living in the 14th century? The town's poll tax record for 1379 has survived and gives a fairly comprehensive answer. In the town itself and the adjoining villages of Bondgate and Aismunderby, tax was paid by 583 people aged sixteen or over, from which it is considered that the total population was around 1,200.

About a fifth of the taxpayers' occupations are listed and of these, the greatest number were concerned with cloth and clothing, with seventeen weavers, several fullers, dyers and cutters as well as mercers (who handled fine cloths), seamstresses, drapers and a hosier. Twenty-eight people worked with leather: skinners, barkers, glovers, thirteen shoemakers and a saddler. Twenty-five were concerned with food, including nine butchers which would suggest that, by proportion, Ripon today should have 100 butchers! Probably some of the butchers, actually listed as 'fleshhewers', were stock-rearers who did their own slaughtering.

Only eight people have specifically 'agricultural' labels: a husbandman, two peasants, a yeoman, a cowman, an oxenherd, a wetherherd (herding rams) and the pinder who rounded up stray animals. However this was a banded poll tax and of the large number on the bottom band, few have their occupations given; most of these people would work on the land, either for someone else or on their own plot.

The fact that one taxpayer in seven was a non-Riponian reflects the known mobility of labour in the years that followed the Black Death. From information in the Minster's accounts for 1354, it is clear that this scourge struck the town around 1352 and in succeeding years, there are many entries in the rent roll of *vacant*, or *formerly in the tenure of*.

The man who paid the most tax was Walter of Leeds, whose job as *ulnager* for the West Riding was to record how many lengths of cloth were sold in the town. His residence here is clear evidence of the town's importance in the trade. By 1520, however, the wool trade had collapsed and a little later the historian Leland wrote that … 'the town fair was much celebrated for cattle and horses'. Perhaps this, and not cloth, was to be the basis of Ripon's prosperity in the years that followed.

Accounting in the modern sense was unknown. The clerk at the Minster who cast up accounts year by year in narrative form thought in terms of dozens or of 'fingers and toes' but had to write down the answer in Roman numerals. Here is an example from a medieval inventory:-

'In total, m'iii^{c}iiij^{xx}viii li xjs ijd'

or £1388 11s 2d

No wonder that errors were so common.

If we allow for the massive inflation that has occurred over the centuries, coin denominations as small as ¼d clearly had significant purchasing power. It amounted to one twenty-fourth of a craftman's wages for a day. The smallest coin then available was likely something smaller, and clipping of coins into bits was common, as was bartering.

At first sight one wonders how people could manage with the coinage available? It has to be realised that at that time most people grew their own food, some made their own clothes, they gathered wood for fuel and made their own simple furniture. They would have been bewildered at today's range of consumer spending. So money had then much less significance in society than it has today.

Reliable weights and measures were essential for trade and a record exists of several being delivered to Robert of Ripon about 1399, by order of the wakeman. They included a *lagena* (about a gallon), *bushel*, *peck* and lead weights, with *unum hoper cum scala*.

As for language, the Minster's records clearly show the difficulties that the clerks had at times with their 'Latin'. In 1321, one referred to … 'Robertus le gaoler man de Ripon', some expenses in 1345 include 'a novo (i.e. new) buket' and mending 'les belousse' (of the organ), and in 1472 payment was made for 'clavis (i.e. nails) vocatis dowbilspikynge'.

A man of high standing for much of the Middle Ages was the wakeman. He had to set the watch at night by sounding a horn and from then until daybreak, was held responsible for the town's security. Householders who had paid him their insurance premium and suffered loss through burglary or fire were entitled to compensation from him. The custom may go back to the time of Athelstan (early 10th century) and Ripon's oldest horn possibly dates from that period.

To end this section concerned with Ripon people, let us take note of some prominent families.

IMPORTANT FAMILIES OF THE TIME

Domesday Book lists 'Cludun' and at an early date, Roger de Clotherum was Member of Parliament for Ripon. Joanna, who was heiress and last of the **Clotherholme** line, married *Sir Randall* **Pigot**, whose successors held the manor of Clotherholme up to the Reformation. A coat of arms bearing three picks appears in various parts of the Cathedral, indicating that the Pigots were notable benefactors. Margaret Pigot's will of 1485 provides a mine of information for those interested in social history. Her gentlewoman Elizabeth Radcliffe was to have her spruce chest and her … 'rede Englishe boke', together with much bedding. At

Figure 3: emblems of three important local families

Ward

Pigot

Mankenfield

Margaret's funeral, six old men were to stand … 'ylkoone holdyng a torch in his hand'.

On today's Ordnance Survey maps, the name of Givendale is associated with three farms, about two miles east of Ripon and one of them was the home of the **Ward** family, at least as far back as 1266. Mary Ward was born in 1585 and founded an order of nuns in Germany. It was inevitably suppressed at the Reformation but was re-founded in the last century and is active today world-wide.

The **Norton** and **Mallory** families both had homes just north of Ripon. Several members of the Norton family were involved in the Rising of the North in 1569, and a writer at the time said that the assembly in Ripon Market Place in November of that year … 'was the most effectual thing the rebels did'. The Norton coat of arms – an ermine sleeve – appears in places, in the Cathedral.

The **Markenfields**, who were related to the Wards, merit attention. John de Markenfield, canon of the church in 1309, was Chancellor of the Exchequer under Edward II. He received the royal licence to fortify his home, Markenfield Hall, which still stands surrounded by its moat. Not long afterwards he was jailed for raping a neighbour's widow but when he was pardoned, he threatened legal action against the Sheriff of York! After the Scots' raids he appears in a worthier light, as one who left money to rebuild the shattered bridges. A chapel in the north transept is named after the family.

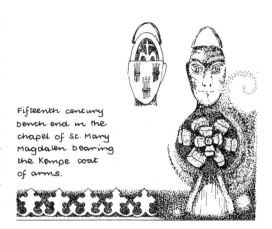

Fifteenth century bench end in the chapel of St. Mary Magdalen bearing the Kempe coat of arms.

THE ARCHBISHOP

Strollers who are in the town's market place at nine in the evening and hear the hornblower *setting the watch* will probably be told the tradition of the *wakeman*, extending back perhaps a thousand years. The wakeman was a man of authority in the town, responsible mainly for protecting commoners' rights and for seeing to the inhabitants' security.

The canons' authority was much greater, as the next chapter will show, but what of the archbishop's? Ripon's attainment of Borough status in the mid-12th century made it an ideal place for the siting of his palace with the shrine, pilgrims and litigants all contributing in various ways to his income. His authority over the canons was not absolute – in a 1228 court case the archbishop's bailiff was found guilty of violating the canons' liberty and was heavily fined. But he did *collate* (appoint) canons and issued licences to *farm out the minster's prebends*, i.e., he authorised the rent collectors. Only one case is recorded before 1300 of an archbishop's visitation, at which he would examine how the minster was being run and the conduct of its staff. There were doubtless others, of which the records have not survived.

Of immediate concern to all the townsfolk was his monopoly over corn-milling. In addition, he had considerable jurisdiction over civil affairs in his manor, which was four miles in radius and much larger than the Canons' Liberty. To back up litigation, he had his own court and prison and could erect his own gallows.

Besides tolls at markets and fairs, he owned mills, property, farmland, woods, livestock and plaster pits throughout the area. In only six months of 1304, from just Ripon, Monkton, Thornton and Whitcliffe, his net income was almost £200, which was the equivalent of a craftsman's wages for thirty years. Farther afield in the county, he owned still more sources of income. His right to demand tolls from markets and fairs was rigorously enforced, as two examples will show.

- In 1366 Richard Tempest, knight, was ordered to explain why at the May and October fairs, he erected pens for sheep and kept the profits and why he had also appropriated the takings at other sheep- and horse-folds, which belonged to the Archbishop. At the May fair at that time, the Archbishop could expect profits of around £12: multiply by about 2,000, to get the modern equivalent.

- Again, when in 1441 the men of the Forest of Knaresborough looked set to challenge his authority and create disorder at the May fair, he summoned 200 mounted men-at-arms from Tynedale and the Hexham area, another 100 from Beverley, Cawood and York and yet more from Ripon and Otley. They united to keep Ripon ... 'like a town at war', and strutted up and down boasting ... 'would to God that knaves and lads of the forest (Knaresborough) would come here so that we might have a fair day upon them'.

If his command of military affairs comes as a surprise, it should be borne in mind that early in the previous century it was the archbishop who – as tenant-in-chief of the King – called the people to arms to defend the country when the Scots threatened.

The role of an archbishop has changed over the succeeding centuries!

CANON POWER

The word *canon* will usually be employed in this book although *prebendary* is more correct in the middle ages. At that time a canon (prebendary) enjoyed the income in rent, tithes and so on of a particular investment in real estate, called a prebend.

Aldred of York is known to have founded prebends in 1060 and this holding of land is listed in *Domesday Book* a few years later. About the end of the century, Henry I declared that the canons' lands were to be ... 'free from expedition and castle work', meaning that they were not under any commitment to the defence of the area, a job which in fact fell to the Archbishop.

To become a canon it was essential to be well-to-do and helpful to be well-connected – in fact, servile birth was a bar to ordination. No ordinary priest could afford to present a rich cope to the minster at the time of collation or, as the rules required, ensure that the stipulated large sum of money would pass from his estate at death, to the church.

Of the 59 men presented by the Pope for Ripon canonries between 1268 and 1411, a few of the 26 admitted were foreigners. In 1301 for example, Johannes, son of Brante Saraceni of Rome became a canon but he was charged a few years later with having obtained the appointment surreptitiously, and with being a married man.

No less a person than the Archbishop of Ravenna also obtained a canonry, but such examples are exceptional. William Langland touched on this scandal in Chapter 8 of *Piers Plowman*.

Names of noble families appear, like Peter of Blois in the late 12th century. He was secretary to Henry II, in high favour with the Pope and cardinals, and was probably related to King Stephen. Stephen le Scrope – nephew to the murdered Archbishop – became a canon in the 15th century, as did William Scrope a few years later: at the age of seventeen! William had a papal dispensation for the appointment and in later life he was simultaneously a canon of both Beverley and Ripon and also Archdeacon of Durham. Another distinguished canon was George Neville, brother to Warwick the Kingmaker.

Many canons simultaneously held high office under the Crown, like Michael de Northburgh and John de Wynewyk who were each keepers of the privy seal. Thomas Haxey had the misfortune to be sentenced to death for recommending economies in the King's household, at some time prior to his appointment (the sentence was later remitted). Alexander Legh (1480) took a warning to Edward IV concerning the defection of John Neville with a body of troops and was later employed by Richard III in surveying the bridge and walls of Newcastle-on-Tyne. Of Edmund Chatterton it is said that … 'little is known of him except for the enormous number of preferments that he received'.

The tenure of canonries was often short, because when canons found that the value of prebends did not come up to their expectations, they would try to exchange them for something better!

Hugh Ashton (Canon, 1521) was associated with Christ's and St John's colleges in Cambridge but John Sendal was not so philanthropically minded: he left enough money in his will for a thousand masses to be said for the souls of himself and his parents. His will included his green cloak furred with beaver and with a hood and other cloaks of buckskin or furred variously with polecat or marten. One is left with no doubt as to Sendal's social status.

The canons were responsible for the spiritual welfare of a huge parish extending many miles westwards to Pateley Bridge, in Nidderdale. By the 13th century there were seven canons and each prebend lay within the parish of Ripon, except for that of Stanwick which was so far to the north – almost in County Durham – that its prebendary normally resided in Ripon and employed a vicar to do his parochial work at Stanwick. The canon of Stanwick was traditionally in charge of music at the minster and at one period also had the grammar school master responsible to him.

After 1301 each prebend was named after the principal village within it – Stanwick, (Bishop) Monkton, Givendale, Sharow, Nunwick, Studley and (Little)thorpe – and it was around that time that serious shortcomings in the canonical system were tackled by the Archbishop.

Canons who were foreigners or civil servants were not residing as they should, and their work was being passed irresponsibly to other people, even laymen. Some canons were themselves laymen or were married, and finally the canons' houses were being allowed to fall into disrepair. The Archbishop ruled that in future the cure of souls within each prebend was to be the responsibility of a vicar and the canons were to be relieved of both pastoral work and the performance of services.

One wonders, what responsibilities did they have! It is significant that there is a record in the next century of a special payment being made to the canon who resided at Christmas, underlining the fact that the responsibility for services was now the vicars'. From 1304, the vicars lived in the Bedern (house of prayer) which Nicholas of Bondgate had given to the church.

Each canon was paid a modest salary but his main source of income was the tithes from his own prebend – hay, corn, wool and lamb – together with some rent from houses and land. Nunwick prebend enjoyed the income of a brewhouse (rented to the Earl of Cumberland), while Givendale yielded a small rent from a mill at Markington. The least valuable prebend was Sharow, worth £16 in 1535, whilst Stanwick was the richest and then worth £40, or about six times the annual wage of a craftsman.

It is hard to grasp the complexity of the minster's staff in the Middle Ages. Of the seven canons, six had a vicar, deacon and sub-deacon in Choir and a proctor in Chapter whose job was to see to prebendal business. The status of the vicars was recognised when the Archbishop insisted that the canons should pay them an extra £2 a year to cover the cost of horses and servants, whilst in the following century, Henry V granted them the right to use a common seal.

So the Choir had to seat seven canons, six vicars, six deacons, six sub-deacons and six choristers: total, 31 people. If we add in the Archbishop who possibly had a seat in the misericord range, the total is 32, which was in fact the number of misericords, up to the 19th century.

The word 'dean' appears a few times in late medieval records, but it means 'rural dean' and not 'dean' as head of the Chapter. Perhaps the church had a dean in earlier times because a canons' court case of 1228 cites the inquisition of 1106 ... 'attended by the Deans and Chapters of York and Ripon'. In later centuries it was customary for the senior canon present to preside over Chapter meetings .

The offences heard in the canons' court related most often to debt and charges of immorality but their jurisdiction was wide. It included adulteration of goods, defamation of character, working on festivals or on Sundays, affrays in church, matrimonial cases, neglect of spiritual duties, perjury, ribaldry, theft, usury and clerical trading.

Normally the clergy were disciplined by the Archbishop but when one of the vicars, Henry Scorton, was known to be trading as a layman he had to appear before the canons: and explain why he had mixed sand with the wool he was selling!

PAYMENTS INFLICTED BY THE CANONS' COURT

In 1308 the Chapter's own bailiff was found guilty of immorality and fined the enormous sum of £20. Two women who had fought in the churchyard – with shedding of blood – were also fined, but penance was a more common penalty. So John Ray found when he was convicted of immorality and sentenced to be flogged five times round the font (which was then near the west door) and the market place; ridicule forming a significant part of medieval punishment. After committing adultery, Robert Nellott had to walk in front of the procession on three successive Sundays wearing only cloak and smock, his head uncovered and a wax candle in his hand. In the days before Human Rights, ridicule was a cheap and effective way of enforcing discipline. The most formidable punishment of all, excommunication, was usually associated with offences against property, as a later chapter will show.

A further aspect of the canons' powers was the measures that they could take, under Athelstan's charter, to ensure the peace of St Wilfrid's Liberty. When John Slingsby and others invaded it and assaulted the household of Sir R. Piggott, they had to walk to church with bare heads and feet, carrying a burning candle in one hand and a naked sword held aloft, in the other. Lawlessness was not uncommon in the 14th and 15th centuries: when six men from Askrigg and Sedbergh invaded the Liberty, armed with lances, swords, bows, arrows, jaks (padded jackets giving protection to the wearer and known to have been in use during the Civil War), steel helmets and Welsh bills, they were summoned to appear in the Chapter House for correction. A friend suggested to me that the wearers ought to be described as armed ruffians.

Little is known about the grammar school at this period. There are several references to rent paid by the schoolmaster or for the school house – which was in 'Annesgate' – but no information as to who attended it, or what they learned.

WORSHIP

The last section outlined the many ways in which people's lives were controlled by the canons. This section will show that religion and adult life were almost inseparable.

In the Middle Ages, 40-hour weeks and annual holidays were unimaginable and Sunday observance had not become a matter for debate.

In 1468, it's true, Joanna Farrard was caught spinning on Sunday and was sentenced to a whipping, but this is a rare instance in the Ripon accounts, of the profanation of Sunday.

The working day was long in summer and short in winter. As to the working week, the chance survival of a carpenter's calendar from the period, containing daily entries of his work, shows that people averaged about five working days a week, after allowing for the many non-working Holy days throughout the year. So the whole nature of the working week was determined by the church.

As one comes to appreciate the hold that the church had over people's lives, one is bound to ask why the Reformation did not occur sooner. The church was presumably strong enough until then to prevent it.

Take *Mass,* for example – it was the most important service, yet the laity were almost excluded from it. They attended regularly and no doubt enjoyed the sights, sounds and smells, but it took place in the Choir from which they were excluded (*except,* as one Archbishop of York had ruled, *for important people*). It was conducted in Latin, which none could understand, and when they did communicate – which usually happened only at Easter and Christmas – they received only the bread and not the wine. Why this should have become the pattern is not clear. They must have had little idea of what it was all about. By 1303 affairs were in such a state that the Archbishop issued a set of rules for the ordering of services and the conduct of clergy and people. One rule stated that *on* Easter Day ... 'the body of Christ is to be delivered to all without any exaction of tithe or due', which reveals that the church had actually been charging for the Sacrament! The custom probably dated back to the time of the crusades, when the sacrament was sometimes withheld from those who had not supported the cause.

The status of the Minster at this time was virtually that of a cathedral, for a bishop of Galloway had been consecrated in it, in 1293. In the same year, there is record of a parish church of Allhallows but it had vanished by the time of Leland's visit in the early 16th century.

In the rest of the chapter we shall look at baptisms and weddings, then go on to review the calendar of a typical year.

BAPTISMS

Because it was believed that the soul of an unbaptised child was doomed and since infant mortality was so high, it was customary to baptise on the day of birth. Perhaps that is why we read in the Ripon accounts of a clerk being paid to fill the font at Easter and Whitsun. The charge for baptism was normally 0.5d (about a twelfth of a craftsman's daily wage). One hopes that it was filled at other times of the year too, but the point is that water, already blessed, was always available for instant use.

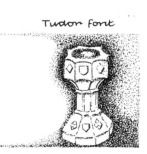
Tudor font

Mercifully, concerning the infants' welfare, the custom of baptism by immersion was replaced, by the 14th century, by that of pouring water over the child's head.

The Norman font formerly near the west door was used for the old rite, whereas the Tudor font in the south aisle was designed for the new mode. Scrutiny of it will reveal traces of the lock, required by a ruling of the Archbishop, to prevent people stealing the water for occult purposes. By custom, the church was presented after the ceremony with the christening gown. It accumulated vast stocks of them and it had been ruled in 1228 that … 'Chrism cloths were not to be put to profane use but made into hand towels, surplices or other things, with all reverence'.

Over two centuries later, the Treasurer appended to his annual accounts a statement of stock movement for the year, which began:-

> opening stock of chrism cloths $cc^{ma}lxvj$ (i.e. 266)
>
> cloths received from baptisms during the year $c^{ma}iij$ (103)
>
> Total $ccciiij^{xx}ix$ (i.e. 389 – which is wrong!)

Such errors are not rare in medieval accounting – not only was the manipulation of Roman numerals difficult, but accounts were set out in narrative form and not in columns. A deficit was called a *superplus*!

Of the 369 cloths, eight were subsequently used for infant burials, nine made into towels, fourteen used for repairing vestments and six used in other ways, leaving a closing stock of 332. For a society that was so far from affluent, this would appear to our materialistic eyes a terrible waste.

Thanksgiving for the child's birth – *churching* – invariably followed. The service has fallen from favour in modern times, perhaps because it is regarded as 'folk-religion'. I recall a churching in the 1970's after which the mother presented the canon with an old sixpence wrapped in silver paper, with the words 'That's for good luck, Father'. One may deplore the act or smile at it – but does the church today pay sufficient attention to thanksgiving? In a society so marked by a lack of courtesies, what more important 'thank you' can there be, than that for the birth of a child? Have we something to learn from the Middle Ages?

Confirmation was usually applied to very young children, but no records of it at Ripon have survived.

MARRIAGE

A full marriage service in church entailed first the exchange of promises at the church door, then mass at the altar steps and finally the sprinkling of the couple in bed with holy water – *purification*. In 1401 there were 36 purifications, at a fee of 4d each (a day's wage for a labourer).

Just the exchange of promises constituted a legally binding marriage pact. Did not Chaucer's wife of Bath declare:

'Five husbands at the church door have I had'?

It had been ruled at Ripon in the 13th century that the promises should be made before a priest, but when the validity of John Outhwaite and Margaret Donning's promises was challenged in 1471 (because Margaret's relatives wanted her to marry someone else), the canons rejected the challenge on the grounds that although the promises had been made in a private house, they were made before witnesses. The promises were in this form:

John: 'Here I take thee Margaret to have to my wife, to dead us do depart and thereto plight I thee my trouth'.

Margaret: 'Here I take you John to have to my husband to dead us do depart and thereto plight I you my trouth' .

Note that John used 'thee', but Margaret, 'you'.

THE CHURCH'S YEAR

Until England adopted the Gregorian calendar in 1752, the *year ended* on 24th March. In different years however, the church's year at Ripon ended – for accounting purposes – on the feasts of St Mark the Evangelist, or the Nativity of St John the Baptist, or St Michael the Archangel, or the Ascension! We shall keep to the 31st December.

With its succession of festivals, processions and drama, the townsfolk were kept aware of the church's constant influence over their lives; lives punctuated not by weekends off, but by Sundays and a colourful succession of holy days. So dramatic a change over the centuries has to be borne in mind if we are to understand what life in Ripon was like in the Middle Ages.

The excitement of Christmas was sustained into the New Year, by the celebration of the *Epiphany* (January 6th), which was marked by a play and a service of blessing the ploughs. In 1484, 11s 7d was received for the ploughs in 'Riponshire', at 1d a plough: that implies there were 139 ploughs.

Candlemas followed soon afterwards (February 2nd: the Presentation of Christ in the Temple, or the Feast of the Purification) but the accounts tell us regrettably little about it. Today, worshippers are presented with candles as they enter church, whereas five centuries ago, they brought their own candles – into which they had pressed coins – and gave them to the church.

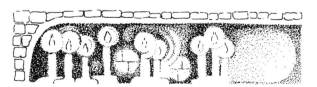

The onset of *Lent* was announced by the ringing of the pancake bell on *Shrove Tuesday*. That reminded people to attend church to confess their sins (shriving) and to use up any meat in their homes in pancakes, in readiness for the Lenten fast.

The bell is still rung today, but not heeded in the way that it formerly was. However, a pancake race is nowadays run along Kirkgate on Shrove Tuesday. Starting from the west door of the church, it is hugely popular, with the Dean among the front runners.

The next day was *Ash Wednesday*. In readiness for it, clerks were paid to burn to ashes the previous year's palms. Parishioners' heads were annointed with ash, because *from ashes you came and to ash you will return* – a custom largely dropped after the Reformation but now coming back into use. From the 13th century, it was customary to cover the altar cross with a Lenten veil and one wonders whether the hooks in the choir pillars, two bays from the east end, date back to that custom? Until the Reformation, the high altar was two bays west of the east end.

Lenten fines exacted from the parishioners formed a substantial part of the church's income, and will be dealt with, later.

For *Palm Sunday*, yellow sallow and ivy were used as palms and were brought from the nearby archbishop's park . On Palm Sunday, the *Gloria* was perhaps sung by the choristers, standing on the ledge high up inside the west front, as was the custom at York. We do know that the Gospel was read at the *Palm Cross* in the churchyard, which is probably the blackened stump near the south-west tower. (Figure 4).

At the *Last Supper* – the day before *Good Friday* – Jesus gave to his disciples a new commandment (*novum mandatum*) that they should love one another, hence the name *Maundy Thursday*. For the minster, the day involved a formidable amount of preparation.

Three bushels of wheat were bought, 'both for Maundy Thursday and for the communion of all parishioners on Easter Day'. Firewood was bought for the oven and two clerks spent six days baking the bread, for which they received an ale allowance as well as their pay – a common practice in the Middle Ages.

Figure 4:

This stump of reused Roman stone still stands outside the nave south aisle. Is it possibly part of the original Palm Cross?

The next purchase was 46 *lagenas* (approximately 46 gallons) of ale! It was spiced with 3/4lb ginger, a pound of sugar (which cost the equivalent of a craftsman's wages for $3^1/_2$ days), 2oz cloves and the same amount of mace (again, great luxuries), a pound of sugar plum, half a pound of sugar cake and 2oz ginger comfit. White wood cups were bought for distributing the spiced ale on Maundy Thursday and $2^1/_2$ gallons of wine were also needed but we don't know who received the wine, and who the ale. The Maundy service was a *distribution* to the laity of wheaten bread and spiced ale and not a communion.

A *Judas* was used in the choir at mattins on Maundy Thursday, Good Friday and Easter Eve and was a triangular candlestick. Fowler suggests that the name was a corruption of *Jews*, the extinction of the candles, one by one, signifying the cruelty of the Jews.

Little information has survived concerning services on Good Friday but there is a reference in 1472 to processions to and from the Easter sepulchre and we know that parishioners communicated from the Reserved Sacrament on that day.

The origins of the *Paschal Vigil* go back to the earliest days of the church. In modern times it is observed either late on Saturday evening or early on Sunday morning and worshippers' candles are lit from the main *Paschal Candle*. In the Middle Ages, this was a gigantic affair. In 1401, it cost £1 10s to make and paint a new stand for the candle, whilst at Durham, the candle was so immense that a special contrivance had to be let down through the roof to light it.

It was common practice on great occasions to pay the members of staff who participated, from choristers and the grammar school master, to the ministers. At Christmas, Epiphany, Easter and St Wilfrid's nativity, ministers – usually fifteen in number – were paid for acting. In 1447, Robert Brampton received 16d for writing the script. What a pity that no details of the plays have survived.

From Easter we move on to *Rogationtide*, the three days preceeding *Ascension Day* (a Thursday). This was the most dramatic period in the church's year.

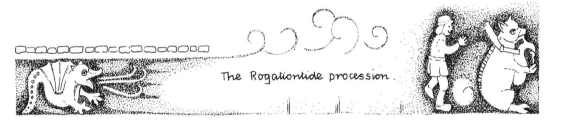

The Rogationtide procession.

On Monday, Tuesday and Wednesday there were lively processions from the minster, through the town and on to the fields. A dragon participated. It was at the head of the procession on Monday, behind the cross the next day and relegated to the rear of the procession on Wednesday, without the stuffing in its tail – signifying Christ's victory over sin. Minstrels enlivened the procession, no doubt carrying bagpipes. A misericord in the Choir shows a pig playing pipes, which perhaps questions whether people enjoyed the noise! The most important feature, however, was the carrying of St Wilfrid's shrine (details of which follow later in this chapter). This was the honour of local knightly families who rented land from the minster. They had to appear in the Chapter House beforehand to confirm their tenure and thereby earn the privilege of carrying the shrine. On reaching the fields, the shrine was housed in a tent surmounted with a cross.

The *grythmen* have been mentioned earlier in the book; they were men granted sanctuary within the Liberty of St Wilfrid, in accordance with the terms of Athelstan's charter. In return for the church's protection, they had to appear in procession at certain times of the year, like Rogationtide, carrying their rods. Six men who failed to do so in 1485 had to appear before the canons in the Chapter House where they were sentenced to be beaten with their rods on the feast of St Wilfrid's nativity: no doubt before an expectant audience.

In 1512, it is recorded that 78s was received from collections in town for *the newly ceilinged part of the roof* in the nave of the church, *for making new the cloud for the Holy Ghost.* Also that year, carpenters were paid *for taking down and erecting the Holy Spirit at Ascension and Pentecost,* and materials were bought for Thomas Payntour to paint it. Ascending and descending angels were very popular in the Middle Ages; one came down and censed Edward IV at his coronation!

A record from 1478 is puzzling at first sight. Until 1604, the town's security was in the hands of the wakeman, who had to set the watch each night, but in 1478 money was paid to *ministers of the town called wakemen, who officiated at the shrine at Rogationtide.* Wakeman means watchman and these particular men were responsible specifically for the shrine alone.

The *St Wilfrid Feast* in August was attended by *minstrels.* Today there is a band, decorated floats move around the town, and everyone finishes up in the minster for a short service. This takes a very different form from its medieval counterpart, as an extract from the responses for mattins then will show:-

> *Minister: Queen Hermenburga, the persecutor of all good men, insolently snatched a box of relics from the man of God (i.e. St Wilfrid) and flung him into prison darkness.*
>
> *Response: But very soon, wearing these same relics, she was possessed with a devil and began to go mad.*
>
> *Glory be to the Father …*

One hopes that the staff celebrated the St Wilfrid festivals cheerfully – there were three in the Middle Ages – because in 1401 they had protested that it was really too much work to put on a memorial service for King Athelstan each month. The great number of festivals in the medieval church was very much in the minds of those who compiled the *Book of Common Prayer* in later years. It has been suggested that it sometimes took longer to find the service in the book than to say it.

What went on at *Christmas* time? In town, the young men made a collection for the church on Christmas Eve whilst within the church the star was filled with wax, ready for use. Christmas was a time when everyone attended mass, even men like John of Clynt who, for his good service to the archbishop in 1377, was excused church attendance except on the greater feasts. 'But', the archbishop added, 'this is not to be taken as a precedent'. The townsfolk were joined by the *foreign chaplains* from chapels and churches in the district, all wearing their capes. Eleven attended in 1493, including one called Benson; a common Ripon surname today. Another had the name of Qwyxley (cf. Whixley, a village near York), which well-illustrates medieval spelling.

What was the colour of the choristers' robes? That may seem a rather pointless question but it was realised in 1982 that our choir wore robes of a colour permitted only to royal foundations; but by whose authority? On learning that the Royal Maundy would be held in Ripon Cathedral in 1985, it was a serious matter! Was there a medieval precedent? A quick scrutiny of the Chamberlain's Rolls gave the following information as to colour:-

> *1478 coloris blodii melly*
>
> *1502 coloristawne*
>
> *1513 rusceti coloris*
>
> *1520 coloris marble*
>
> *1525 coloris lez Russett*

none of which, regrettably, had any bearing on the royal red: even 'blodii melly' is a blue and not a red, mixture. Hopes then turned to James I: when he gave a charter to the minster in 1604, did he authorise the royal colour? It was an anticlimax to discover that the Dean and Chapter had changed the colour from blue to red as recently as 1908 – and certainly not by royal authority!

So a different colour had to be used in future and the new robes (red, but not royal red) were worn on Maundy Thursday 1985, in the Queen's presence. It is amusing that when the Cathedral choir is on vacation, services are often sung by visiting parish choirs who sometimes flaunt the forbidden colour, or something very similar to it.

Now back to the ceremonial of the Middle Ages and to the shrine. The earliest known shrine is that of Archbishop Oswald towards the close of the 10th century. Over two centuries later, Archbishop de Grey – the man responsible for the church's west front – had a new shrine made, ornamented with silver and gold.

It was found that no bones were missing but the head was enshrined separately (on 26th December 1224) and probably kept behind the high altar. Where the body itself was placed is not recorded. In Archbishop Oswald's time it had been placed at the most northerly point of the church then standing on the present site.

Around 1520, extensive and very costly work was done by the Ripon woodcarvers and others in making a new high altar and shrine, work that was still in progress two years later. It is not absolutely clear that this shrine honoured St Wilfrid but, in any event, nearly all the work was lost in the Reformation.

At a shrine, not only money and valuables were presented; a record of 1470 seems to relate to wax models of cured limbs being offered – a custom that has survived in the Eastern Church to the present day.

CHURCH ACCOUNTS

The fact that our country has Chancellors of the Exchequer today, stems from the practice in the middle ages of working out accounts on chequered cloths or boards – moving counters from area to area as additions or subtractions were made. In the first edition of this book I gave worked examples but the process is so complicated I have omitted it from this edition. The original accounts contain many mistakes which, considering the complexity of the process, is no surprise; they worked in units of **m, d, c, l, xx, x, v** and **i**.

In buying and selling, notches were made on a tally stick which was then split lengthways, with one strip for each party. That occurred for example in 1470, when Robert Barber made and sold to the church … 'xiiij dd (i.e. fourteen dozen) candles as shown on the tally stick'.

Figure 5: showing the chamberlain's receipt over a series of years

Year	1410	1439	1540	1551	1553
Tithes	45	40	38	37	37
Lent fines	32	23	42	39	33
Easter offerings	6	5	6	5	6
Associated with death	23	16	8	3	3
At the shrine, various rents and masses	34	15	1	0	0
Rents	5	4	3	2	2
Totals	145	103	98	86	81

Mistakes could easily occur; thus in 1551, the Chamberlain recorded his total receipts as £408 15s 9^1/$_2$d whereas the correct sum was £88 15s 9^1/$_2$d. He had confused iiij^{xx}viii with ccccviii. Small errors are common.

If we consider the finances of the church itself, as distinct from the finances of the prebends, the accounts that have survived are:-

26 fabric accounts between 1354 and 1520

4 treasurer's accounts between 1401 and 1484

17 chamberlain's accounts between 1410 and 1557.

and it is difficult to assess the overall financial status of the minster. The chamberlain's account received by far the most money of the three. From 1410 to 1553 its total receipts varied widely, but Figure 5 gives a few of the individual amounts, in pounds.

The table in figure 5 shows that the income in the chamberlain's account fell from £145 in 1410 to only £81 in 1553. Such was one consequence of the Reformation. Bear in mind that one must multiply the figures by at least 2,000 to get present-day equivalents.

The first three classes in Figure 5 were not markedly affected by the Reformation, but notice the drop in income from deaths and at the shrine. And in 1553, £66 was paid to Walter Dynham who was rent collector for the Duchy of Lancaster, to whom the assets of the former Collegiate Church now belonged. Clearly, little income was left for the minster.

The income from all three accounts in 1410 (*fabric, treasurer's* and *chamberlain's*) was approximately equal to the wages of a top craftsman for 24 years. About half of it was spent on payments to the ministers. Many of the accounts that have survived are damaged and it is difficult to form a clear picture of staff salaries. In 1439, for example, the prebendaries of Monkton and Thorpe each received £19 and in 1447 a similar sum was paid to the prebendaries of Givendale and Stanwick, much more than was paid to the other men. The reason for this is not known.

Figure 5a: annual Fabric Account income – 1393 vs. typical years

Year	Typical of period	1393
Money boxes in church	£7 to £10	£1
Money taken at St Wilfrid's nativity	£1 to £1.50	nil
Custodian's salary for year	No figure	£11.54
Balance carried forward	£20 to £25	nil

Some of the smaller expenses are interesting – organ repairs (including several hides), a big rope for the well, three men washing relics, wax for the Chapter seal, rushes for the floor of the Chapter House and Choir, grease for the bells and candles for the sexton to help him on winter mornings.

There is a very odd feel to the Fabric Account for 1393-4. Consider the figures in Figure 5a for annual income. Is it merely coincidence that, in 1393, work had begun on a new and expensive house for the chapter, on the south side of the church? The section began with sub-standard maths and ends with questionable accounting.

DEATH

Try to imagine yourself in the Ripon of 1352. So long as people can remember, everything that happens – including death – has been accepted as God's will. The church, after all, determines not only how people will live but what they will believe.

Black Death suddenly strikes the town. Within months, about a third of the population is dead. Churchill, writing of this time, said that … 'The church was grievously wounded in spiritual power. If a god of mercy ruled the world, what sort of rule was this?' The prospect opening before the church was disturbing. Was its right to mould people's belief about to be challenged? Its teachings left no doubt concerning the torments that awaited sinners in the next world, indeed death itself was personified in the most gruesome ways in the church plays.

So wise people kept their account with the church in credit. The church was usually the recipient after death of one's best possession and Ralph Pigot for example left it his 'Mercedes': 10 oxen with an iron-framed wagon. It was common to leave money for anniversary masses, whilst both fees and donations flowed into the church's coffers at funerals.

In earlier times the great abbeys had prospered substantially from benefactions, but as they became more worldly, people transferred their charity to the parish churches. As the last section showed, such giving fell sharply at the Reformation. The minster would no longer receive 15s.8d (perhaps £1500 in modern money) for 47 memorial masses for a deceased archbishop, or money for the 1,000 masses prescribed in a former canon's will.

If we close with medieval wills, it will highlight the enormous change in people's attitudes to death in the last half millenium. The will normally began with a declaration of the testator's soundness of mind then continued:-

> 'In the first, I bequeath my soul to God almighty
>
> and to his blessed mother St Mary
>
> and to all the saints in Heaven'

Spiritual matters came first; worldly, second.

SEEDS OF DESTRUCTION

Some years before the Reformation, Wilfrid Holme wrote a long poem that poured scorn on some of the superstitions that the church had so profitably exploited, like ...'St Wilfrid's bone of Ripon to keep cattle from pain, And his needle which sinners cannot pass the eye'. This is the only reference I have found to St Wilfrid's bone, but his burning iron features a few times in the church accounts. It was perhaps used originally for ordeal by fire which the church had banned in 1215, but was kept by the canons and used for branding cattle. In 1419 it yielded 33s 4d and in 1503, 105s 11.5d: set that against a craftsman's daily wage of 6d. The *needle* was the hole in the wall of the Saxon crypt, said to have been used as a test for chastity.

Relics, too, exemplify the church's exploitation of the ignorant and the credulous. 'They were often kept', wrote Batsford and Fry, 'in emporia stocked with human scraps of all kinds, as unattractive as they were often unsavoury'. Staff at Ripon were paid periodically to wash the relics!

Indulgences were so discreditable a feature of the medieval church that Moorman ignored them altogether in his authoritative book, *A History of the Church in England*. Sinners were often sentenced by the church to extended periods of punishment that included segregation in church and compulsory fasting. When the church hit on the notion of selling release from the very penances that it had imposed, its immediate wealth was assured and equally, its ultimate ruin. Thirty indulgences were granted at Ripon in 1338, such as for repairing the fabric, and many similar cases occurred in succeeding years. One Archbishop promised indulgences to all who would listen to a great friend of his preach at Ripon.

Several entries in the early 16th century accounts relate to laymen buying indulgences for large sums of money – clearly to sell at a profit – and one entry summarises indulgence fees received at Ripon for the entire York diocese. Another mentions the *pardon of St Wilfrid in the provinces and dioceses of York, Durham, Carlisle and Ripon*: the almost-Cathedral status of the minster has already been referred to. The thought of laymen building up investment portfolios of indulgences is horrifying.

Although great numbers of people went on pilgrimage to Rome to earn indulgence, there is no record so far as I know of Ripon people doing so, but Agnes Snelle of nearby Kirkby Malzeard was discharged from serfdom in 1380 so that she could make the journey.

Records of *excommunication*, the church's ultimate sanction against the ungodly, reveal the medieval church at its very worst and like indulgences, Moorman ignores the subject entirely. Even five centuries on, the formula pronounced against offenders makes the blood run cold:-

> *You are cursed within and without, in roads, in country, in the house and outside it,*
>
> *eating, drinking, asleep, awake, coming, going, standing, sitting, everywhere.*
>
> *You are excommunicated, damned, anathematised, for ever.*

I wonder how our Lord would have regarded the custom of excommunication – and to whom was it applied? It was threatened by the Archbishop in 1320 *on all who violate my park*: his lordship's fury over the damage inflicted on his property during the Scots' raids is all too clear. A few years later the Archbishop actually placed the Bishop of Durham under excommunication, following a dispute over their respective areas of authority. The only time it is known to have been applied in Ripon is by the canons, after some 'sons of Belial' had smashed open the canons' gaol, armed with axes, chisels and hammers, in order to release clerks charged with homicide. It appears that the church's ultimate spiritual punishment was used only for temporal crimes.

THE END?

The canons managed to retain their collegiate status until nearly the end of Henry VIII's reign, but the last two or three decades were not happy ones.

The earliest record in the Ripon accounts of Henry exacting a subsidy from the church was in 1524, but when he threatened (after 1531) to end the independent jurisdiction of Papal courts, the churches had to pay retrospective fines over five years for having allowed English matters to be settled by foreign (i.e. Papal) courts. The sum at York is known to have been vast but unfortunately no financial records for Ripon have survived for the years 1532-1539.

Lion's head water spout. West front.

Until 1534, only the treasurer had a key to the Chapter House and when in that year, Christopher Dragley (as treasurer) used this privilege to impede chapter business, it was clearly time for the rules to be changed. Three years later an injunction from Fountains Abbey specified that in future the Abbot of Fountains was to have two keys. How had such a remarkable change come about, in the relations between the minster and the abbey?

To answer that question we must consider the last days of Fountains Abbey and, especially, the part played by Marmaduke Bradley. Bradley was for a time both Abbot of Fountains and a canon of Ripon and comes down to us as a most unscrupulous man. He enters our story in the year 1535. Thomas Cromwell's commissioners had accepted the resignation of the current abbot of Fountains, William Thyrske and in passing the news to Cromwell, added that a monk called Marmaduke Bradley, who had been left a prebend in Ripon church, 'was the wisest monk in England' and would pay Cromwell £200 to be made Abbot of Fountains. £200 was a huge sum of money (perhaps 30 years wages for a craftsman), and Bradley saw it as too good a chance to miss. Indeed after retirement at the abbey, his pension was £100 p.a. (Note that in later years, any attempt to purchase office within the church was illegal. Until recent years, new canons being installed at the cathedral had to take the *simoniacal oath*, swearing that they had not offered money to gain their appointments.)

When Bradley did become abbot, he ordered his predecessor, at a month's notice, to present a complete set of accounts for his period as abbot. This Thyrske refused, and he asked Sir William Mallory of Ripon to obtain the King's support for a pension for him. Bradley immediately delivered a counter-blow, through Cromwell.

Bradley eventually surrendered Fountains Abbey to the crown in 1539. He had already become a canon of Ripon in 1535 and from 1554-1556 was the only canon residentiary at the minster. Besides being paid for those duties, he also received a pension of £100 a year from the abbey! So he recouped his investment in just two years.

It is hard to assess Bradley's character because we know neither the full financial picture, nor the social and ethical standards of the day, against which his contemporaries would have judged him. Undoubtedly though, it must have been humiliating to the minster not only to receive orders from the abbey but ultimately to have the former abbot in charge.

Just before Bradley became residentiary, the sacristan was disciplined for failing either to ring the service bells or to fill the wash basin (probably the one outside the Chapter House door): who could blame him? The minster was about to lose both its collegiate status and most of its possessions. Why worry about not ringing a bell or two?

This chapter has ignored such major factors leading to reformation as anti-clericalism and anti-popery, on the grounds that we simply don't know their significance in the Ripon of the early 16th century. But there must have been many who wondered, like the neglectful sacristan, 'Is there a future for the church in England?'

These events prompted the late Dean, Edwin le Grice to write this poem about Bradley. He gave me a copy in his own handwriting:

MARMADUKE BRADLEY

(A poem by Dean Edwin le Grice)

'If you commend the unjust steward
Commend me too.
I share his acuteness, astuteness,
civility, ability to look ahead, to make a plan and put it into action.
Like him, I understand the mysteries of the money market,
the changing price of property and people.'

'If I'm elected abbot', I said to Cromwell,
'a thousand marks first fruits, I'll pay your royal master
Within three years:
But for yourself, take time, take your pen, sit down,
Write quickly,
Six hundred on the day:
No borrowing, no delay!
Mammon makes no fine distinctions between gambling and investment
When this world's friendship is at stake'.

Abbot of Fountains I became
And standing here preside
As the last chapter of this tale is told,
Its fountains flow no more.
Brave men, those abbots -
Jervaulx, and my predecessor here:
Making their pilgimage of grace - - -

Brave indeed, but lacking this worlds wisdom!
Worse than the burning fiery furnace
The penalties they suffered.
Like the gospel steward
I know my limitations -
I cannot dig; to beg I am ashamed; I am a trained Cistercian
Content to keep my profile low, my manner plain;
I do not share the hubris of the Huby tower:
I have no desire to wear a Tyburn martyrs crown.

When all else fails I know what I shall do:
I'll settle for my canonry at Ripon
Carefully though all vicissitudes -
Thorpe Prebend in the lovely gate of High St Agnes,
mastery of the Hospital of Saint Mary Magdalene:
respectability, domesticity,
even modest generosity;
and at the last
a quiet minster grave.

If you commend the unjust steward
Commend me too.
Children of this world are wiser in their generation
Than children of light.

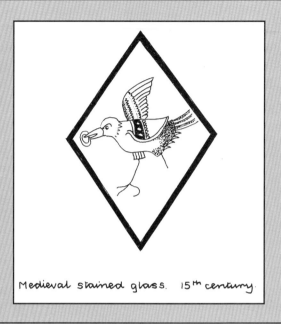

Medieval stained glass. 15th century.

Two examples of medieval art in Ripon (see also Photo 32, p.186)

Wall painting from the Cathedral.

CHAPTER 5

Turmoil

(1547-1660)

BY GOOD FORTUNE, several records have survived relating to Thomas Blackburn, whose service at the minster spanned parts of the reigns of Henry VIII, Edward VI, Mary and Elizabeth. Sufficient information exists to enable us to see, through Blackburn's eyes, many of the changes that occurred from 1540 to 1570, corresponding roughly to the early period of this chapter.

At the beginning of his ministry, he had the distasteful duty of collecting fines imposed upon the church by the King, a job which would, if anything, have increased his commitment to the old Catholic ways.

That was about the time that Henry caused the *Valor Ecclesiasticus* to be compiled. For Ripon, it listed all receipts and payments of the Collegiate Church, the medieval hospitals and the many chantries, both within and without the church, which was described as being in the diocese of Chester and the county of York.

In 1546, Blackburn was a chantry priest at the minster. When Edward VI became King in the following year, the prebends and chantries were all swept away following the publication of the Chantry Certificate (for which the *Valor Ecclesiasticus* provided valuable information). The endowments passed to the Duchy of Lancaster and it was said that … 'there are only seven, six or five ignorant ministers left, who had only small allowances'. The total presumably included Blackburn, who had a yearly fee of £2 as supervisor of the fabric and a further £2 as treasurer. He was responsible for all 'goods and jewellery', as well as for handling some of the tithes due to the King. Some years later we know that he bought the bread, wine and ale needed for the Maundy Thursday service, but without the former luxuries of spice and sugar.

Blackburn probably regretted the freedom granted priests to marry in Edward's reign, and would have been shocked at the banning of vestments and the new custom of letting the laity receive the cup at mass, a practice forbidden for the last three centuries. Assuredly, he would not have welcomed hearing the epistle and gospel read at high mass in English and not Latin.

It is hard today to comprehend the turmoil of the period covered by this chapter. The endowments which had been confiscated in Edward's reign were restored in Mary's, seized again in Elizabeth's, partly restored in James', confiscated by the Parliamentarians and restored for good in 1660 (Gowland). Acts were passed in the reigns of Edward, Elizabeth (two) and Charles I ordering attendance at church on Sundays, as a means of eliminating dissent. In practice, Acts of Parliament, persecution and civil war all failed to achieve this end, whether the *dissenters* were Catholic, Protestant, Puritan or of other kinds.

Mary's reign (1553-1558) followed and offered mixed blessings: the old Catholic ways were restored but at the cost of a horrifying persecution of *heretics* (i.e. non-Catholics). No Ripon people, so far as we know, were caught up in the persecutions: that was to follow in Elizabeth's reign (1558-1603).

When it began, Catholic dissenters were the focus of suspicion and, in 1567, staff of the church at Ripon were disciplined because they had hidden away 49 Catholic service books in a vault during Edward's reign . Thomas Blackburn and John Brownfleet alias Carver were ordered to read the lessons at morning and evening prayer in the body of the church so that people could hear them. The two men were also accused of taking the sacristan's keys one night and of hiding stone from the demolished altars in the church. (Perhaps it was some of these stones that Sir Gilbert Scott found in his restorations late in the 19th century). Blackburn and Brownfleet admitted the charge and were also accused of secreting 'six great tablets of alabaster full of images' within a vault: these would be the late 14th century tablets of which a few fragments have, mercifully, survived (see Photos 16, p.173, and back cover).

Whellan recorded in 1871 that during alterations in the choir 'a few years ago', the carvings of a bishop, the Coronation of the Virgin and the Resurrection were found near the Dean's stall and about three feet below the surface. We are fortunate in having these objects intact today. Another of Blackburn's colleagues, John Birkby, was in trouble for very different reasons. He had appeared in church dressed in 'indecent apparel – great breeches cut and drawn out with sarsenet and taffeta and great ruffs laid on with laces of gold and silk'. On a holy day, Birkby appeared at worship without a gown but with a long sword by his side. John Jackson too was in trouble because he had made altar breads bearing a crucifix.

It is clear that by this time it was not merely liturgical discipline that was under strain, but discipline in general. At York minster for example, Oswald Atkinson had been birched as a punishment for playing football inside the church one Sunday. Brawling, drunkenness and disorder had become features of the times; so how much has life changed?

On All Soul's Eve in 1568, Thomas Buck admitted going round Ripon with the under-sexton and begging money and candles for the ringers. With some of the money they bought ale to drink in church and with the rest 'they did bestow good cheer abroad in the town'.

Blackburn (see above) was in trouble of a different kind that year. Having been ordered to stop up St Wilfrid's needle and to take down the stone altars, he admitted that he had not done so and confessed to 'idolatry and damnable superstitious worshippings (meaning churchings) in the Lady Loft in times past'. He denied removing images from the church in order to protect them.

Much more serious trouble broke out in the following year, 1569. Mary, the Catholic Queen of Scots who was seen as a threat to Elizabeth, was then a prisoner at Bolton Castle a score or so miles away and a natural focus for the Catholic aspirations of many in the area. She had an ally in Christopher Norton of nearby Norton Conyers, who secured a job as guard at the castle and helped to plot her escape. The plan was for Mary to dress as one of her servants and Christopher to be her swain but the plot failed. Mary was removed southwards and is said to have spent a night at Thorpe Prebend house (on the south side of the church) on 26/27 January, 1569.

A crucial event was the assembly at three in the morning on 18 November 1569, in Ripon Market Place of fifteen hundred well-appointed horsemen and a large number of footmen (most of them unarmed and brought there by coercion). This was the first step in what was to be known as the 'Rising in the North', one writer describing it as ... 'the most effective event of the rebellion'. News spread rapidly, and at York boats were ordered to stay within city limits and the ferry boat to be ... 'either sonken or otherwise kept at the discretion of Mr Beane'. The Lord Lieutenant ordered that ... 'whenever any alarm shall happen within York, no manner of men, women or children shall make any showting, crying or noysem but to keep sylens'. I wonder how the staff at the minster reacted to this tumultuous situation?

The setback did not deter Norton's family. Christopher's father, 'Old' Norton, was sheriff of Yorkshire at the time and used his knowledge of the county to the full in plotting the Rebellion of the North which followed.

Most of his nine sons took part, as did his nephew Thomas Markenfield (his family was mentioned in Chapter 4). Even Norton's daughter helped; she had made the banner used at the rallying of forces in Ripon market place. Old Norton had supplied the intelligence for the muster; the Earls of Northumberland and Westmorland supplied the arms and supplies.

From Ripon the rebels swept northwards into Durham. At the churches they encountered, Protestant service books were ripped up or burned, wooden communion tables smashed in pieces and local people were compelled to restore the old stone altars. Thomas Blackburn was a not-unwilling participant at Ripon, for on 13 March of the following year, he was found guilty of saying mass at the time of the rebellion, and of hearing 'other popish services'. Fined £6 13s 4d, he was ordered to do penance – together with Chris Baldersby, clerk – in a white sheet over his usual dress. A few days later Jackson, Foxe and Thomson of Ripon were also arraigned. Foxe had borne the cross at the rebellion, at a procession sung in Latin 'being forced to do so' by the rebels: note again, coercion.

At Barnard Castle, the rebels captured the Castle. An excavation there in modern times suggested that some of the rebels had sabotaged the water supply to the castle to bring an end to the siege, during which a great many men had jumped over the ramparts, to meet either death or serious injury. Just seven weeks before Blackburn's arraignment , Sir George Bowes had carried out the Queen's instructions to 'make the examples great in Ripon and Tadcaster'. Making a circuit from Thirsk, he accomplished 600 executions. Undoubtedly many of the Ripon victims had been compelled to join the rebellion by their superiors. How did Thomas Blackburn view that, one wonders? Was that when Ripon's Gallows Hill got its name? - it's about a quarter mile south of the cathedral.

The Earl of Northumberland was eventually beheaded in York whilst Thomas Norton was hung and quartered at Tyburn in the presence of his nephew Christopher. Christopher was hanged next but the butcher cut him down and disembowelled him while he was still alive. The penalties inflicted were for treason and not for religious dissent: not that that makes them appear any less barbarous, to us.

The miseries of the rebellion did have one very positive consequence. Elizabeth realised the part that ignorance had played and a watch was kept in future on the diligence and ability of the clergy. So, because of their unfitness for office, the curate of Pateley Bridge was committed to the castle at York and the schoolmaster at Ripon, John Nettleton, was discharged. Later in Elizabeth's reign plans were formulated for a college at Ripon. They lapsed, but were revived in James' reign.

A Papal Bull of 1570 excluded Protestants (and specifically Elizabeth) from sovereignty. Anglicanism had already been established for a number of years but old problems remained. In 1580 a commission

at Ripon found that many people were staying off work on the old holy days, which did not feature in the new prayer books. Absenteeism from church led to two acts being passed towards the end of the century and one consequence was the execution for heresy of Peter Snow of Ripon and other men from the Ripon area. Four centuries later these Elizabethan martyrs were canonised in a service at St Peter's Rome, which was attended by many people from Yorkshire and Durham.

Towards the end of Elizabeth's reign, lack of order extended to the churchyard as well as the church and the vicars were instructed to 'clean it up or be fined 6d (2.5p) for each default'.

Having noted that in the Middle Ages the clergy were instructed to give the sacrament to the laity without charge, it is surprising to find that, in 1590, the laity were obliged to make a yearly payment to the Minster, in respect of bread and wine consumed at the Eucharist.

The succession of James I (1603-1625) brought new hope to the church and he quickly granted it a charter (in 1604) restoring its collegiate status, with a staff of six canons and for the first time, a dean. But full restoration of the church's endowments proved difficult. The church petitioned James in 1605 for the means of implementing his charter and it was only in 1606 that a dean, canons, singing men, organist and choristers were all restored. The collegiate church had at that time the right to fine or imprison its officers.

There were high hopes that plans for a college at Ripon, first put forward in Elizabeth's reign, might now be realised. A detailed specification was prepared including staffing, number of students – about 500 were envisaged – and timetable, which began:-

> *Weekdays:*
>
>> *5-6 am: public prayer*
>>
>> *6 am: Hebrew, Syriac, Arabic*
>>
>> *7 am: physics, algebra*
>
> *and on Sundays:*
>
>> *5-6 am: public prayer in Hebrew*
>>
>> *6-7am: ditto, in Greek*
>>
>> *7-8 am: ditto, in Latin*
>>
>> *9-10 am: divine service in English*
>>
>> *10-11am: sermon in English*

– a schedule demanding a very tough breed of student. Regrettably, no money was available and the plans were dropped, never to be revived.

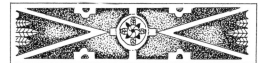 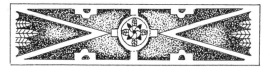

Border adapted from the Fowler monument.
Date: 1608.

Non-attendance at church was still a problem and it was ruled at Ripon that ... 'Inhabitants shall keep their street doors shut upon every Sabbath and festival day during all the time of divine service and sermon and not suffer any person to drink or play at unlawful games in their houses'.

James' intolerance of Catholic recusants led to the Gunpowder Plot, commemorated in the *Book of Common Prayer* until at least 1820, which gave thanks for deliverance from ... 'Popish treachery and the most traiterous and bloody intended massacre by gunpowder'.

At the end of Elizabeth's reign there is a record of Moses Fowler, preacher and he later became the first dean of the new collegiate foundation. Fowler's successor is better known because he – Anthony Higgin (Figure 6) – established at the minster the superb collection of books (now housed at the University of Leeds Brotherton Library) intended to constitute the college library. It contained many rare hand-written volumes as well as a Caxton. On the lighter side, Higgin's will reveals that he left his oldest hat and a shirt to the vicar of Pateley Bridge. Only a decade or two later, the effigies of both Fowler and Higgin were to be vandalised by the Roundheads, who also smashed most of the doors and windows in the church. In Charles I's reign (1625-1649) another law was passed compelling attendance at church, this one being directed against Puritans. The dignity of worship was fast deteriorating and Archbishop Laud found it necessary to order altars to be kept clean and to prohibit cockfights in church.

Figure 6: This bust of Anthony Higgin (Dean from 1608 -1624) is still displayed in the Treasury, The head and hands were removed in the period of Roundhead vandalism.

Plague struck the town in 1625 and the sub-dean at the time, John Bramhall, comes down in the records as a faithful and caring pastor ... '*He showed his exceeding great love to his flock in staying among them in the time of a most contagious and destructive pestilence, visiting them in their houses and baptising their children'*. The plague was so bad at one point that baptisms were carried out in the fields. Later, Bramhall was active in the organising of the church in Ireland, where he became Primate in 1660.

Rules for the Chapter were first drawn up in 1635, a year in which the vicars and singing men were ordered to attend to the preacher and not go to sleep. The Dean's salary is recorded as £93 a year; the verger's, £3.

Before Charles' reign ended in 1649, worship was in further turmoil and, under the Covenant of 1643, all men over the age of 18 were bound, in effect, to eliminate the established church. It had already been terminated in Ripon. Around that time a 'Dr Richardson' was a preaching minister (Presbyterian-style) at the Minster, and his wife is commemorated in a plaque mounted on the wall of the choir south aisle. That same year, the Commonwealth introduced its *Directory of Public Worship* to replace all previous service books and there used to be a copy in the Cathedral library. The sacraments were proscribed, the altar became subservient to the pulpit and the elimination was ordered from churches of all images and idolatry – again. A 'Mr Edward Robinson' was preaching minister from 1655-6, and Presbyterian worship continued until Charles II's reign began in 1660.

Throughout the period being considered (1547-1660), there was a bewildering sequence of change and counter-change as attempts were made to control whatever was considered the dissident group of the day. After the Reformation, change had become endemic as more and more groups professed to follow the true faith. The momentum was unchecked by legislation, persecution and abolition of the monarchy; it merely flowed into new channels.

In the first part of the twentieth century, schoolchildren would sing of the *vicar of Bray,* who repeatedly trimmed his professed faith to suit the requirements of the day. To the children it seemed rather silly, but to the Thomas Blackburns of the time, it was horrifying.

THE TOWN

In studying the late Middle Ages in Chapter 4, we looked at the town first and the church second. The church and its customs changed little during that period, and the aim was to establish the backcloth against which the church's worship and routine were enacted. The period we are now considering (1547-1660) presents a complete contrast, with events in the town sometimes the consequence of developments in the church: the Rebellion of the North is an extreme example. The medieval church had completely dominated the town and when in Tudor times it showed signs of disintegration, the normally well-ordered pattern of town life also suffered. Fines were imposed in the Queen's court for simple things like not keeping water courses clear, allowing the churchyard to become a tip and failing to remove dunghills in the streets.

In 1577, John Atkinson was fined 3s.4d for harbouring 'unlawful guests' and John Cooke was in trouble for ... 'entertaining and harbouring suspicious persons in his house contrary to the law'. It is not known whether this infraction referred to Catholic recusants or to restrictions operated by the trade guilds: in 1598 the Town Book ruled that strangers might only lodge in Ripon on production of testimonials from two JP's and similar restrictions on foreigners were confirmed in James I's reign.

The town no longer made woollen cloth but the leather trade continued, lace-making was established and, in James I's reign, spurs were made here. That last industry is commemorated in Ben Jonson's phrase ... 'as true steel as Ripon rowels', so was clearly well-known, at least in the north.

William Wray was Ripon's leading citizen (the Wakeman) in 1584. He was a prosperous merchant with a shop in town and his account books contain much of interest to the historian. In 1586 he sold John Mallory (later Sir John) 7lb of gunpowder and a few years later Lady Mallorie bought currants, raisins, prunes, ginger, litmus and red sandalwood from him. Lawrence Edward bought a hogshead of prunes and a barrel of sweet soap; Sir William Mallorie of Studley Roger and Hutton Conyers, *Russet jeans*; George Dawson (to be mentioned later), *fustian. Linen cloth, buffin* (a coarse cloth used for gowns), Spanish silk, taffeta, coloured silk and *hairy buttons* were just a few of the many commodities available to customers. In October 1601, Wray received a large sum for equipping the soldiers who took part in Mountjoy's conquest of Ireland, and one can admire the wide range of his business interests.

Some coin catalogues do not list an eighth of a penny but at one point, Wray had to work out the cost of 3s $\frac{1}{8}$d per week, for a year. Extension of prices was a thankless task, and for one sum Wray and his father got different answers because one assumed the noble to be worth 4s, the other 6s 8d.

Mary Ward, who founded an order of nuns in Germany, was born about this time (1585). She presented personally to the Pope her case for establishing an active – as opposed to a contemplative – order for women but was unsuccessful, and was later imprisoned in Munich by the Inquisition. Her father Marmaduke owned lands at Mulwath, Givendale and Newby (east of Ripon) and was related to a family implicated in the Gunpowder Plot. Her birthday was celebrated worldwide in 1985, and I met here nuns from Peru who had never before left their own region. A German television crew came to record the occasion, but British television ignored it! The Ward coat of arms is present in both the Markenfield Chapel (off the north transept) and on the stone screen under the central tower.

Concerning the office of wakeman, one feels that William Wray would have fulfilled it with diligence. By 1598 however, there had been many disputes concerning both the election of wakeman and the competence with which he carried out his duties. A Town Book was therefore prepared, signed by William Mallorie (who had been one of the Council of the North under Elizabeth) and William Ebor. It seems that a major cause of difficulties was the huge size of the town council, all of them elected for life ... 'Some were sick, some were feeble and some just plain awkward'! Although the church's grip on the town was waning, and local people pressing hard for freedom from its domination, the book notes that any dispute concerning election of the wakeman was to be reported to the Archbishop.

George Dawson, a wealthy York merchant, was *fee farmer* to the church from 1597-1633, responsible for letting out the church's estates and collecting the income; he married the daughter of Sir Stephen Proctor. Proctor had earlier bought the Fountains Abbey estate and had used stone from the abbey to build Fountains Hall, which is now owned by the National Trust. It was he who in 1604 had conducted an inquisition into the state and value of the minster's former prebends, then owned by the Duchy of Lancaster.

Thorpe Prebend House in High St Agnesgate is on the site of a much older house. Dawson took a lease in 1607 on the present house, in which James I is said to have stayed twice: he was presented on the second occasion with a set of spurs (Ripon was then famous for their manufacture). A memorial to Dawson – six strips of latten (a brass-like alloy) – was formerly on the wall of the south choir aisle, but they were removed earlier in the present century (Figure 7).

Before the end of James' reign, the Bedern (a house of residence for cathedral staff) in Minster Road had been demolished. A new house was built on what became the site of the Deanery (now the Old Deanery Restaurant).

Charles I stayed in the town on the way to his coronation in Edinburgh in 1633, but Ripon was to have much less happy associations for him. Seven years later, the Scots invaded and caused such panic in Yorkshire that people rushed out of churches during services. In order to bring an end to hostilities, the English and Scots met at a house near Ailcey Hill (now gone) and signed the *Article for cessation of arms as agreed at Ripon 26th October 1640*, which was an ignominious surrender.

Three years later, during the Civil War, Roundheads commanded by Mauleverer had failed to take Skipton Castle, on the roof of which Lady Anne Clifford had had cannons mounted. The troops set off for Ripon, pursued by Sir John Mallory. Great damage was inflicted on the Minster before Mallory's soldiers arrived … 'to make the Roundheads feel the points of their swords' ,and it was many years before the church was restored to order.

Figure 7: Fragments from a memorial to George Dawson.

The strips appear to read:

'His nature mild, his mind devout,
His wealth the poor well fed,
So dead, he lives in spite of death
And grave,his fatal bed.
Whom lately Sheriff, Mercheant free,
York's wealthy city had;
And former chief of Rippon Church,
Now Rippon mould hath clad'.

A local man who served Charles I with distinction during the Civil War was Jordan Crosland, of Newby. At first he held Helmsley Castle for the King, and then secured an honourable surrender by which the defenders were allowed to leave bearing armour and weapons and Crosland took command of Scarborough Castle. Like Richmond Castle, it has the distinction of never having been taken by force. A memorial to Crosland in the south transept records that he served as colonel to both Charles I and Charles II.

For two nights in 1646, Charles I was in Ripon as a prisoner. Five years later – Charles by then executed – Riponians had a brief glimpse of Cromwell with his army as they moved rapidly from Scotland to Worcester. Cromwell must have remembered the occasion, for he later granted the town the right to have a fair, every other week.

Three years later the Protectorate ended and Oliver Cromwell's brother-in-law was about to become the most brilliant Dean in the Minster's history.

CHAPTER 6

Change and decline
(1660-1836)

IN 1660, THE MONARCHY WAS RESTORED, the Bible in English had long been available throughout the land, a new prayer book was in preparation for all Anglican churches and capital punishment no longer awaited those with dissident views. Did this augur the start of a happier era for the church?

In medieval Ripon, church and state had been inextricably linked. The concept that church and state were one was an inherent premise of the subsequent 1662 *Book of Common Prayer*. Authority in the medieval church devolved downwards from archbishops, to bishops and then to parish priests. Such a hierarchy was abolished in the Commonwealth of Oliver Cromwell, when detailed rules were laid down for the conduct of services, aimed at eliminating traces of the old, Catholic ways. The dean, Thomas Dod, had to resign and for several years, Ripon had no dean until the appointment in 1660 of John Wilkins (who was actually Dod's cousin, and brother-in-law to Oliver Cromwell). Before restoration of the old Catholic ways some priests had emigrated, while others had been obliged to adjust their ways and probably their beliefs too, according to the new demands of the state.

Wilkins was an unusually gifted man. A doctor of divinity, he was involved in discussions at Oxford with Christopher Wren the architect (who knew Charles II well), Robert Boyle the physicist and others of prominence. It was from such a gifted group of men that there was born the Royal Society of England, the first such society in the world. Wilkins not only conjectured that man might one day fly (probably unaware of the earlier, similar thoughts of Leonardo da Vinci) but went on to speculate as to the inhabitability of the moon.

In view of Wilkins' friendships at Oxford, it comes as no surprise that a former chaplain to Charles II – William Lloyd – was appointed canon at Ripon in the same year as Wilkins took up office. The name of the verger then is not known, but a dispute occurred as to whether he was a fit person to have a key to the main doors to the Choir. The earliest named Dean's Verger is Christopher Darnbroke in 1688 and it is not until 1836 that the name of a Canons' Verger is recorded, one John Hardcastle.

Religious intolerance was still strong. The Baptist John Bunyan was in prison for most of the time that Wilkins was Dean and in 1663 at Ripon, some Quakers were victimised for their beliefs and were put in gaol for three months.

In the following year the new mayor, Sir Edmund Jennings (who was MP for the town at one time) instructed the churchwardens and constables to 'repress indecorous conduct on Sunday, walking in the nave after service had begun and playing at games in the churchyard – which had now become common'. It should be mentioned that after the Restoration, all church services were held in the Choir. Nationally, church-attendance was causing concern and a new Act of 1664 made it illegal for anyone over the age of 16 to worship, except according to the customs of the Church of England.

The mention of Edmund Jennings recalls an incident which well illustrates one facet of life at that time. His younger brother Jonathan had high words with a Mr Aislabie of York after a gathering at the Duke of Buckingham's house in that city. Jennings accused him of affronting the daughter of Sir John Mallorie, probably the Mallorie involved after the sacking of the minster by the Roundheads. Jennings killed Aislabie in a duel and immediately went in the Duke of Buckingham's coach to London, where he secured the King's pardon! A few years later, Jonathan Jennings presented to the minster two superb silver gilt chalices with matching covers, still kept today in the Cathedral Treasury. The John Aislabie concerned was father to the John Aislabie who is mentioned later in this chapter.

In 1663, the 'Dr' Richardson who had been a preacher at the minster during the Commonwealth was involved in the Farnley Wood Plot which was a conspiracy for overturning the government. The conspirators planned to march successively on Leeds and London but the King's soldiers surprised them and took prisoners. Richardson managed to escape, probably to the Low Countries.

The population of Ripon and Bondgate at that time was approaching 1,700.

Little is known of Wilkins' successor John Neile, except that during the Civil War, he fled for safety to Scarborough Castle. He asked to be buried … 'privately in the church of Ripon near the closet (i.e. Chapter House) door where we put on our surplices'. In many churches the floor provided an indoor graveyard with premium rates for interments and Ripon was no exception. It was a custom much deplored by the picaresque Yorkshire novelist, Lawrence Sterne.

Most of the wooden coffins beneath the minster floor are now mere dust, but the Mallories and Aislabies rest undisturbed in their lead coffins.

Neile was dean for only a year and the next man, Thomas Tullie, had an even shorter tenure of office. A zealous Calvinist, he had previously been chaplain to Charles II (like William Lloyd). Thomas Cartwright followed in 1675; and was ... 'slavishly obseqious to the ruling powers: in rebellion, after the Restoration and in the reign of the Catholic James II'. As in the song about the vicar of Bray, a zealous high churchman was he and so he got preferment. While he was Dean, the Corporation petitioned Charles II ... 'that the statutes of King James and Queen Elizabeth against Popish recusants be retained'.

Lawrence Hornsby became parish clerk at the same time as Cartwright became Dean and is the earliest named holder of the office. In those days parish clerks played a prominent and very audible role in worship, one which evidently amused the novelist George Eliot, to judge by her treatment of the parish clerk in *Silas Marner:* parish clerks were then renowned for their stentorian voices.

Immediately the Catholic James II had fled the country, Catholics throughout England were summoned to take the prescribed oaths and in Ripon those so affected included Lady Mary Tancred, Francis Wyvill and George Markenfield, all of Allhallowgate.

Sir Edward Blackett was commemorated after his death by a fine memorial in the minster and he is also noted for having given to the church portraits of Richard II, Catherine of Aragon and Anne Boleyn. At the close of the 17th century, Blackett was working the mines in Allendale (north Pennines) for lead. His business so prospered that he engaged Christopher Wren to choose the site and prepare designs for his new home, Newby Hall – about four miles south east of Ripon. Blackett became MP for Ripon, and Defoe recorded that he bred fine black cattle. In recent years Newby Hall has gained prestigious awards for both house and gardens, something that would have surprised the Victorian historian Walbran, who described the hall as 'this cumbrous pile, recently restored'.

When the Hon. John Byng attended evensong at the minster one Fair Day at 3 pm, he recorded that ... 'The church was filled by all the holiday people, hooping and hallooing; nor was one in the choir but myself, a reader and a clerk. So being quickly scandalised at this irreverence and at the ill-judgment of opening the church on this evening, I departed'.

Byng visited many churches across the country and often found that services were conducted in a slovenly manner. Bishops and Archdeacons lived princely lives and were out of touch with parish priests who were ill-trained, underpaid and often absentees.

Was Ripon's new Dean in 1710 typical of the times? Heneage Dering was born into a Kentish landowning family and as a young man, he saw James II taken by the rabble at Faversham as he was about to leave for France. Two years later, Dering saw the French fleet at anchor in Romney Bay after their victory off Beachy. At the age of 37 he took his doctor of laws degree, 11 days later he was ordained deacon and in the following year became Archdeacon of the East Riding! He went more than once to London – usually on horseback – and stayed in the Lord Almoner's lodgings at Whitehall, ... 'the pleasantest room in London, with one window looking down the Thames and another up the canal in the park'.

On being nominated Dean of Ripon, Dering was installed by proxy; soon afterwards he married the daughter of the Archbishop of York, and it was 19 months after his installation before he actually took up residence in the Deanery (now the Old Deanery restaurant).

An interesting survival is one of his account books which reveals among other things that he paid his charwoman 4d a day and spent 13s 9d on a box of tobacco – equivalent to the charwoman's wages for 41 days of toil..

As to what he contributed to the worship of the minster, very little is known. In 1737 the minster had its first Confirmation service for very many years and if it conformed to the usual pattern of that time, would have been a pretty disorganised affair with hundreds of candidates: 2,400 attended a service some 60 years later.

Holy Communion was celebrated much less often then than now, but at the minster there were celebrations on the first Sunday of the month, Christmas Day, Palm Sunday, Good Friday and Easter Day – when there were commonly a thousand or more communicants. Several of the nearby villages never had a celebration and at Hutton Conyers an agreement was reached whereby the villagers could attend services at Ripon – on payment of a fee!

Two 18th century Aislabies are commemorated in the south transept. When John Hobson visited Studley Park in 1725, he found a hundred men at work on canals and waterways for … 'Mr Aislaby (sic), one of the Directors of the South Sea': John Aislabie was in fact Chancellor of the Exchequer at the time of the South Sea Bubble. He was mayor in 1702 and had become MP for Ripon in 1695, together with Jonathan Jennings (nephew of the man who had killed Aislabie's father). His son William was MP for all the latter half of the 18th century and Ripon owes its obelisk in the market place to the two Aislabies, John and William.

Heneage Dering was succeeded as Dean in 1750 by Francis Wanley who had an inauspicious start. The sub-dean and three canons alleged through their lawyer that Wanley had caused them to be locked in the Chapter House. Wanley was Dean from 1750 to 1791 but fled Ripon in 1780, leaving the Chapter finances substantially overdrawn. When he did return to the town, he found that Canon Waddilove was living in the Deanery and refused to vacate it! Wanley was obliged to take up residence in a house that he owned in Kirkgate, where eventually he died. His memorial tablet fell off the wall during Sunday service one day in 1860 and was not replaced, suggesting that he was held in no great esteem by the Chapter of the day.

It comes as a relief to turn to a great man of the 19th century, Beilby Porteous. His father Robert can be connected by later marriages with both Queen Elizabeth II and George Washington, and had 19 children of whom Beilby was the last but one.

Both Robert and his wife were natives of Virginia but came to England to secure better education for their children. Young Beilby attended the Grammar School at Ripon. Later, when Bishop of Chester, he encouraged the new scheme of Sunday schools in each parish and he was active in the House of Lords on behalf of slaves in the West Indies. He became Bishop of London and campaigned successfully for the stricter observance of Good Friday. There is an armorial panel in the library window in his memory.

About this time, John Wesley had started holding meetings within the Church of England aimed at encouraging a greater sense of commitment among its followers and more reverence in their worship. In 1780 he came to Ripon and sadly the local Methodist Church overlooked the anniversary in 1980. Had Wesley come to the minster a few years earlier, he would have heard prayers being said for success against the rebellious American colonists.

It was customary in those days for the choristers to distribute apples to the congregation at Christmas, a practice that was revived in recent years.

One of England's most-quoted epitaphs comes from that time and is to be seen in the churchyard at the north-east corner of the church:

Here lies poor but honest Brian Tunstall,

he was a most expert angler, until Death,

envious of his merit, threw out his line, hooked him,

and landed him here the 21ˢᵗ day of April 1790.

Robert Darley, who was born in Boroughbridge, inherited Robert Waddilove's property and assumed his name – a not uncommon practice at that time. As Robert Waddilove, he was Dean of Ripon from 1792 to 1828 and is mainly remembered today for the several imposing memorials in the church to him and his family, but he did in his lifetime give over £1,000 to augment clergy incomes. A Fellow of the Society of Antiquaries and Member of the Royal Society of Sciences at Göttingen, he spent much of his time on literary research in Spain. As with some of his predecessors, little is known of his involvement in the life and worship of the minster beyond the fact that in 1825, he was one of a group who petitioned the mayor to support MP's who were opposed to Popery. Perhaps he was present when prayers of thanksgiving were offered in the minster for victories against the French at sea and on the Nile.

An interesting record has survived of the Holy Week 'perambulations' in Waddilove's day. The choir and vicar met at 10 am on Monday, Tuesday and Wednesday, together with the Blue Coat boys bearing branches of plane or 'sap tree'.

They did a comprehensive walk of the town streets singing psalms and stopping frequently for readings. Finally they processed round the churchyard chanting the Litany, and so into church. 'And then went home to get our dinners — if we had any', as one of the choristers wrote. When Easter was cold and wet it must have been an ordeal.

Life expectancy was poor. A memorial tablet (Figure 8) in the nave commemorates nine-year-old Henry Strickland who died after just eight days at the Grammar School and Henry Nesbit (recorded on a plaque nearby) survived only three weeks at another school in town.

At the turn of the 19th century Ripon's population was around 3,000, the town imported its first hogshead of sugar and the architect Wyatt designed the elegant building that is now the city's Town Hall. Wyatt's name became infamous for his 'restorations' at Durham Cathedral and Pugin dubbed him … 'This master of architectural depravity!'

It was probably Dean Webber (1828-1847) who abolished the observance of Candlemas, a service which had caused an 18th century writer to marvel at the ancient church, alive with candle light. The service is now a popular feature of the minster's calendar; Gowland has described Webber as 'consistently disliking anything of interest' and Webber certainly stopped the Rogationtide processions but he cannot have been a happy man. Of his several

Figure 8: Detail from a wall plaque in memory of 9-year old Henry Strickland, his early death in 1818 indicated by the broken snowdrop.

children one died in its cot, one was killed climbing in Switzerland and another was killed by a 'fire machine' — presumably, a railway engine.

A meeting was held in 1829 to consider the expediency of lighting the minster by gas and this was actually done in the following year. But much bigger problems soon loomed and the architect Edward Blore was engaged upon extensive restorations to the fabric.

At about this time, Newman, Pusey and others were active in what became known as the Oxford Movement, dedicated to attaining higher standards of worship.

Newman was initially anti-Catholic and indeed once wrote to a friend 'pray do tell me what a chasuble is?' but in later life, joined the Roman Catholic church. One wonders what views – if any – Webber had on the subject?

In 1833, Dean Webber and his canons were the recipients of a scathing attack in the *Leeds Mercury* on the subject of tithes. It wrote:

> *The people of Ripon, in addition to the usual very heavy tithe upon corn, hay, turnips etc have to pay 5s (25p) to the Dean and Chapter for every milch cow they keep ... ... there are about 1,400 milch cows ... ... which produce £350 p.a. This milch cow tithe was never exacted before the last few years. How is this?*

I have streamlined the original ponderous invective of 1833, which is remarkably similar to that used in one of Anthony Trollope's novels of the same period.

For the Dean and Chapter, worse was to come. In April 1834, the same newspaper had an article stating:

> *BIRTH – TITHE OFFERINGS. At Ripon, on Monday week, of a son, Ellen, the wife of William Darnbrough, tailor in Blossomgate, who is the industrious cottager that was sold up by auction a short time back, by the very revd the Dean and Chapter of Ripon, for various oppressive and vexatious tithes upon his milch cows and etc, and the memorable sale of whose cottage utensils amounted to 2s 7$\frac{1}{2}$d (about 13p today! – author) a full account of which we gave at the time of the sale. This is their tenth child and we understand the parents have quite resolved to christen it Tithe. It is also in contemplation to send Master Tithe, in the course of a few days or so to the very revd the Dean and Chapter as an Easter offering.*

The affair must have done immense harm to relationships between church and community; and that just two years before the church was raised to the status of cathedral. Even when, in 1975, I entered a local shoe shop to buy shoes suitable for wear in the Cathedral, the sales assistant said: 'You stole our church'.

Tithing was still big business in 1846 for the Dean and Chapter instructed their solicitors to press the Leeds and Thirsk railway for compensation for loss of tithe income, following construction of the railway past Ripon and a further half century would elapse before tithing was ended. A few families paid tithes until well on in the next century; but only as a courtesy and not an obligation.

We have overshot the period of our chapter. In 1836 slavery was recently abolished throughout the British Empire and Trades Unions were becoming established in England. Dean Webber and his colleagues had – we hope – ceased to smart from their lambasting by the *Leeds Mercury*.

They were poised expectantly for the ceremony and celebrations that would mark the transition of their great church from minster to cathedral, with a diocese extending northwards to the River Tees, westwards to the moors and southwards to Leeds, Bradford and Wakefield (today, Bradford and Wakefield are themselves dioceses).

Detail from the 18th Century Weddell memorial

C H A P T E R 7

The new Cathedral
(1836-1900)

Late in his reign, Henry VIII had plans for creating many new cathedrals but little came of his intentions and it was not until 1836 that England gained its first cathedrals since the Reformation – Ripon and Manchester. A few years later, Ripon became a city. The new diocese comprised parts of the dioceses of Chester and York (see also the end of the last chapter). The foundation for the new bishop's palace was laid in 1838.

Trollope's *Barchester Towers* gives some idea of the kind of life led by the first bishop, Charles Longley. His salary was £4,500 a year, while the town clerk of Ripon was earning £60 a year.

Longley had a remarkable career being successively Bishop of Durham, Archbishop of York and Archbishop of Canterbury, within six years of leaving Ripon. Longley's effigy is on the right of the stone screen across the church, below the centre tower. Robert Bickersteth succeeded him and is noted, among other things, for missing a train at Leeds on his way to an engagement at Wakefield and securing a lift in the cab of a passing goods train! The fine glass of the west window was given in memory of Bishops Longley and Bickersteth. William Boyd-Carpenter followed Bickersteth and often preached to the Queen. When asked by a friend how he did it with so much composure, he replied ... 'I preach to the scullery maid and so the Queen understands me'. In the window in the nave north aisle, given in his memory, one of the characters is said to have the features of a well-known boxer of the day, recalling the late Bishop's interest in the sport.

Under a new Act early in Queen Victoria's reign, the prebendaries were styled canons. The number had been six under James I's charter but was reduced to four in 1858. They lived during their quarterly residences in the Old Hall, at the junction of Church Walk and High St Agnesgate, then moved to The Residence, which formerly stood where Cathedral Close now is.

The name of the Dean at the end of the century – the Hon. William Henry Fremantle – is perhaps a little intimidating. As human in fact as anyone else, he and the Archdeacon succumbed to the new craze of bicycling. Unfortunately on one outing, the Dean's front wheel caught in a rut, he collided with the Archdeacon and finished up on top of him! Given the formal dress then worn for such pastimes and the abysmal state of the roads, the two must have looked an awful mess.

The Bishop's Palace, Palace Road. It's first occupant was Charles Longley, Bishop from 1836-1856.

THE CITY

No visitor to the City today can remain for long unaware of its claims to antiquity. Indeed, had he seen a letter from the College of Heralds in 1875, he would expect it. The writer describes Ripon as … 'a city second only to York and before all other Municipal Boroughs'. Indeed, the church had been a cathedral in Saxon times, so who would dispute the words of the College of Heralds?

The year 1886 marked the 50th anniversary of the minster again becoming a cathedral. Knowing the considerable showmanship, imagination and industry that the Victorians brought to plays and pageants, is it likely that they would feel great enthusiasm for a mere 50th anniversary?

Suppose that Ripon really had been given a charter in 886, what celebrations could be made in 1886! I'm sure that's how Ripon's 'Millennium' was invented in Victorian times. If one realises that a local antiquarian of the day described the Danes as invading Ripon in the early 14th century (I refer to Tuting and not to the eminent Walbran; Tuting was confusing the Danes with the Scots) one suspects that for the average Riponian of the time, historical niceties (like centuries) were superfluous. So for well over a century, Ripon claimed to be England's second oldest town with a royal charter.

By 1836, thatched dwellings in the town were becoming a matter of the past and Ripon had several schools, but sanitation was horrifying. It was very densely populated and as one citizen wrote:

> 'in many of the confined yards, the liquid filth from the privies and dunghills is allowed to drain through the walls and either to remain in pools upon the surface or to trickle down among the paving stones'.

A simple small drain in the Market Place received both surface water and common filth from all the household drains, ... 'the depth of which is several feet above the level of the cellar kitchens', as a local man protested at the time. Little wonder that the new bishop's residence was built over a mile out of town.

WORSHIP, AND CHANGING WAYS OF USING THE BUILDING

Dean Webber witnessed the transition from town to city and from minster to Cathedral but so far as worship is concerned, he is noted only for abolishing Candlemas and the Rogationtide processions: Candlemas had been forbidden in 1571, but was revived at some later date.

Beyond Ripon, the Tractarians sought a more devout approach to worship. Originally very conservative they later introduced customs that had been discontinued at the Reformation. Indeed, after Pusey had built St Saviour's church at Leeds, where among other innovations, daily mass was celebrated; the Bishop of Ripon described it as ... 'the plague spot of my diocese!'

At Ripon, little changed. Charles Dodgson, who was a canon here in 1852 (his son was 'Lewis Carroll'), wanted the Cathedral to hold a daily afternoon service but this did not happen until 1876. Most people – like Queen Victoria – received Holy Communion only twice a year and Dodgson pressed for more frequent celebrations but there, too, I think was unsuccessful.

The huge numbers attending confirmation services in the 18th century have already been mentioned and the custom continued into the 19th century. Francis Kilvert recorded in his diary that at Hereford in 1870, the bishop followed the new custom of confirming only two at a time, kneeling at the altar rail: but even so, the curate was confirmed in error!

Whatever defects our own Cathedral's programme and customs may have had, people went to church Sunday by Sunday in large numbers. In 1891, the numbers attending morning, afternoon and evening services were respectively 500, 400 and 500.

Figures fell in the nineteenth century but in 2010 they are rising significantly.

Until the Reformation, the congregation were excluded from the choir. We have little knowledge of worship in the minster in the ensuing century but in Charles II's reign, pews and galleries had been crowded into the choir to accommodate the large congregations then attending. During William Fremantle's time as Dean (1876-1895), arrangements changed again with Sunday evening services now held in the nave. Perhaps during Gilbert Scott's re-ordering of the choir a few years earlier the congregation, being obliged to move out of it, had developed a preference for nave services. An extreme example of how the use of the building has changed is that of the undercroft below the Chapter House, formerly: *The Bonehouse*.

When visiting Hythe church in Kent some years ago, I was surprised to see, in an undercroft, row upon row of skulls. Over a hundred years before that, a Mr Francis Buckland (antiquarian and humorist) had been to Ripon, and marvelled at a similar sight there. He wrote:

> *Leaving the Chapter House, the verger conducted us to the crypt which is beneath it. Unlocking the massive door, we at once beheld a 'Golgotha'. Bones were everywhere; skulls, arm bones, leg bones, skulls of old men, young men, women and children. The walls of the crypt are hidden behind a stack of bones six feet high and four feet thick. In former times they were scattered all about the vault but in 1843 the old sexton undertook the task of arranging them. He placed a row of skulls on the floor, then a row of arm and leg bones with the round ends protruding, then another of skulls and so on, till the space from floor to roof was fully occupied … … the pillars of the crypt were ornamented with festoons of skulls … … wherever there was a vacant space, a skull had been placed.*

By carefully counting the skulls on show, he got a total of 9,912 but was dumbfounded to be told that there were still more below the floor, to a depth of four feet. In September 1867, Buckland added a sad postscript to his story … 'I regret to learn that this crypt is now closed to the public by order of the local authorities'. And not before time.

The reader will wonder how such an accumulation came about. The most likely explanation is that when aisles were added to the nave in the early 1500's; it necessitated excavating an area of churchyard which had previously been used for interments, and the bones so disturbed had to be housed elsewhere. The Fabric Account for the year 1512-13 has survived and relates that a mass was celebrated in the nave of the church … 'for the foundation of new work on the south side' – i.e. preparation for a south aisle. Later in the year, the account notes that 24s 6d was paid … 'pro expensis circa cariag le bones'.

The bones were probably then (or later) placed immediately east of the east wall of the choir and hidden by a high wall, which is depicted in a late 18th century engraving at Newby Hall.

After the wall was demolished early in the 19th century, the bones were next accommodated in the undercroft, as Mr Buckland discovered.

The bonehouse windows were not glazed in those days and the youths of Ripon would dare one another to slip in after dark and take a skull. One such skull was used, it seems, as a lathering bowl by a local barber and this caused the novelist Harrison Ainsworth (a contemporary of Charles Dickens) to write a poem about it. A sample of the work illustrates the kind of humour then fashionable.

The barber went to bed one night leaving the skull on a bedside table - - –

> ' But he soon started up in a terrible fright,
>
> Lo, giving the curtains and bedclothes a pull,
>
> A ghost he beheld – wanting half of its skull!'

The poem continues with the spectre clapping on its missing brainpan and vanishing. For a while, Harrison Ainsworth was held to be a worthy rival to Dickens, but we can see why posterity has decided otherwise.

The Ripon antiquarian Tuting wrote caustically of how some churchwardens wanted the Dean to close the Minster Yard. … 'because forsooth the people go in (i.e. to the bonehouse) without paying' and on one occasion, the verger did a quick dash out of the south transept door and told Tuting … 'I have stopped these gentry peeping without paying'.

Francis Buckland's visit here, his account of it and Ainsworth's dreadful doggerel tell us much about how people have changed and even more, what is (or was) considered a worthy use of the Mother Church. For many decades after Buckland's time, the undercroft was still little more than a store but today it is a chapel, which is in regular use.

PEOPLE

In surveying memorials in churches, one inevitably learns more about the great than about the ordinary: Elizabeth Garnett (d. 1921) was neither. As the 10-year-old daughter of a Yorkshire clergyman, she attended a memorial service for railway navvies killed in an accident and for much of her adult life she strove fervently for their souls.

The men lived in temporary camps that were squalid, cold, wet; the accident (and mortality) rates were appalling and the men sought relief in drunkenness and immorality.

It was much easier, Mrs Garnett found, to persuade the men to accept the simple pleasures of the mission huts (cocoa, draughts, dominoes and books for the few who could read them) than to change their near-brutish natures. Her self-imposed calling yielded few tangible results and one must admire her selfless devotion.

Earlier in the period of this chapter, two Ripon men died, each with notable careers.

Commander John Elliott (responsible for building Holmefield House in Harrogate Road, Ripon) had circumnavigated the globe as a midshipman in the Resolution commanded by Captain Cook and he was later present at 'Lord Rodney's glorious action' in 1782. He died in 1844 and his memorial is near the font in the nave south aisle.

Five years later, there occurred the death of Lt Francis Waddilove, a descendant of Dean Waddilove. The inscription on his memorial on the north wall of the north transept is remarkable:

> 'he fell the victim of a long march, about 250 miles, from Lahore to Rawul-Pindee during the very hottest period of the year when according to the register kept in the Surveyor-General's office the temperature reached 100F daily at noon in the shade'.

His brother was a Lieutenant in the Royal Navy and had died a few years earlier, off the coast at Valparaiso.

The son of the Ripon canon, Charles Dodgson, ensured the Cathedral earning a small place in the literary world of the day. His son Charles Lutwidge Dodgson ('Lewis Carroll') would be well acquainted with the fanciful medieval carvings in the choir. On the easternmost north bench end is a monkey, used to symbolise greed and envy and the young Charles would know that the adjacent seat is allotted to the new mayor of the city, on taking office each year. In the carved seat nearby, a griffin chases a rabbit and another rabbit disappears down a rabbit hole: this undoubtedly supplied ideas for his 'Alice' stories and 'Alice' herself has a Ripon origin. When somebody showed Dodgson a photograph of little Mary Badcock, whose father was principal of Ripon College in the city, he realised that she would be the ideal model for 'Alice', and obtained permission for her photograph to be sent to the artist Tenniel, who used it to produce the illustrations for Dodgson's stories.

IN RETROSPECT, 1836-1900

Canon Dodgson's unsuccessful attempt to introduce daily evening service highlights the conservatism of the times although the bonehouse story does make one wonder whether the authorities were not so much conservative, as inert. But can one fairly judge one period retrospectively by the criteria of another?

It has to be said that the Dean and Chapter at the end of the century possessed one enviable asset: a gratifying Sunday head count.

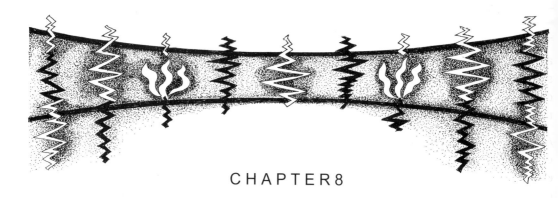

CHAPTER 8

The twentieth and
early twenty-first centuries

THE ONLY NOTICEABLE EVENT IN the first half of the twentieth century was the provision of electric lighting. Until Godwin Birchenough became Dean in 1941, the style of church services had changed little from the previous century which, in a sense, only ended around 1945.

So many changes have occurred since then that it will be helpful to classify them and the reasons for them.*

PEOPLE HAVE CHANGED

In 1901, the congregation begged the Cathedral to provide umbrella stands because on wet days, the nave floor was awash with water. Most of the congregation lived in the parish, they walked to worship (and of course to work) and they knew their neighbours. Life today is different and to try and bring people together they are, for example, encouraged to greet people sitting near them during the course of the principal Sunday morning service and to drink coffee with them in the Cathedral afterwards – practices unthinkable in 1901.

WORSHIP HAS CHANGED

In the second half of the century, the church placed increasing emphasis on the Eucharist (Holy Communion), which is today the most popular Sunday service.

> *Editor's note: Bill Forster's text in this chapter is unchanged from the 2nd Edition of 2010, but by 2018 a number of significant additions and improvements have been made. These are listed in the Foreword, on pages 3-4.

The precise form of service has changed many times to reflect new theological outlooks and encourage greater participation by the congregation; young people often play a significant role in it. Until the 1940's the Eucharist was celebrated by a priest wearing cassock, surplice and hood; then vestments were introduced. The text has been changed repeatedly.

A high standard of singing continues at all services, with the men singers and either boys or girls (occasionally both). On the first Sunday of the month, the singing is led by a newly established music group, with singers and instrumentalists of all ages; congregations are growing steadily. The Easter Vigil was introduced many years ago on Easter Eve; the pattern and content of Holy Week services has changed a number of times in recent years.

CHANGING IDEAS AS TO SUITABLE USES AND LAYOUT OF THE BUILDING

Until the early twentieth century, the nave was filled with beechwood chairs. When oak pews were introduced, the chairs were moved to storage outside the church. When, later, stacking chairs were bought, the beechwood chairs were disposed of.

During the first part of the twentieth century, communion services were all held at the high altar, except for some smaller celebrations for which a chapel had been created in 1914 in the choir north aisle. Half a century later, the choir south aisle was similarly converted. The first major change in the nave was the installation in 1936 of an altar beneath the centre tower. In the 1960's it became the focus of the newly-introduced parish Eucharist, which grew rapidly in popularity and is now the best-attended service of the week. When it became necessary in 1973 to move the nave altar westwards because of repairs to the tower above, it was realised that the new position was in fact better and an altar has remained there ever since.

Since the 1970's, there has been a big increase in the number of 'non-worship' events in the Cathedral. The 1936 altar and its associated choir stalls did not fit this new pattern of use, so were replaced in 1989 by a new altar and sectional, portable, choir stalls which have greatly increased the flexibility of the church.

Until the middle of the century it was unthinkable at Ripon that one should pay to enter the Cathedral, for whatever purpose. But today charges are made (or donations invited) for attending concerts, recitals, festivals or various 'secular' activities. The reason is that - quite apart from the pleasure they give to participants and to the audience - each of these incurs a cost which should be supported by those enjoying the event, and this extra income has so far helped the Cathedral avoid making charges for admission to the building - as many cathedrals now do.

Portable staging and stacking chairs were first acquired in 1972, facilitating a much wider range of activities in the Cathedral. The change, introduced by Dean Edwin le Grice, marked entry of the church into a new era; one unimaginable earlier in the century.

All the new furniture was accommodated in the choir north aisle. So far so good. Then it was decided (against protests from antiquarians) to convert the Saxon crypt into a treasury. But after a few years, the protesters won the day, and all the furniture in the choir north aisle had to be moved into ugly temporary stores (unbelievable!) in the north and south transepts, so as to accommodate the treasury in the choir north aisle. At that point a local benefactor stepped in and funded the creation of the fine new staircase from the south transept to the library, with storage space beneath.

The Saxon crypt is now refreshingly uncluttered and the treasury has been - for the second time in recent years - accommodated in the library. Not a very edifying chapter in the church's history!

Finally, in 2009, the old pews were replaced by oak chairs made by a local firm and the result is one of elegance - and comfort. Neat racks of folding, stacking chairs are in frequent use as well, for busy occasions.

CHANGES TO HEATING AND LIGHTING

When oil prices rose dramatically in the 1970s, heating was only applied from Saturday night until late Sunday afternoon in the winter, and weekday daytime temperatures were often little above 5°C. A new gas boiler installed some years ago greatly improved matters and now (2010) it too has been replaced by a pair of more efficient units.

Until the 1970s the church was lit by a formidable number of tungsten filament bulbs. In 2009/2010 under the name 'Vision Project', all of the electric wiring was renewed and new lighting installed which is much more cost-effective, more versatile and more in sympathy with the Cathedral's ambience. The rewiring included the clocks, the organ, public address system, loudspeaker system, fire alarms and the induction loop for the hard of hearing. Thanks to a local benefactor, floodlights were installed in 2010 covering all the outside of the building. This uses the latest low-energy bulbs, which give a dramatic impression of the building at night as one approaches it, whether from far or near. In truth, one can sometimes learn more about the church at night in the floodlights, than one can in daylight.

The new internal lighting can be used to dramatic effect in services like the Nine Lessons and Carols, with computer-controlled dimming or raising of the lighting.

CHANGES IN THE ORGANISATION OF THE DEAN AND CANONS

It was not until early in the twentieth century that the canons resided permanently within the city and so were available full-time for Cathedral duties. From 1941, the Dean became vicar of the Cathedral parish, a responsibility previously exercised by subordinates. In recent decades, Residentiary Canons have simultaneously held archdiaconates or other diocesan appointments, whilst staff members often help at neighbouring churches, as the need or opportunity arises.

CHANGING WAYS, IN CITY AND CATHEDRAL

At the start of the twentieth century, one of the biggest events in town was the annual Whit Walk when all Sunday School scholars, Non-conformist and Anglican, marched into the Market Square. After a short service, the Anglican children processed with their banners along Kirkgate to the Cathedral. Sadly, this no longer occurs.

From 1899-1902, English soldiers were engaged in the Boer War in South Africa and the Revd J. G. W. Tuckey was chaplain to the garrison besieged at Ladysmith. He eventually became Assistant Chaplain General to the Forces and later, a canon at the Cathedral.

When World War I began (1914), Ripon was rapidly transformed into a huge garrison town, with a site sweeping around Ripon from north-west to south-west. It had its own railways and a population equal to several times that of the city itself. Between the two World Wars, there was standing room only at the annual service at the beginning of November in honour of the war dead and several decades later a packed nave is normal for the occasion. Ripon is still a garrison town.

Frederick Llewelyn Hughes was chaplain in World War II to General Montgomery during his victorious North Africa campaign and rose to the rank of Chaplain General to the Forces. Montgomery himself, by then a Field Marshal, visited Ripon more than once to stay with his former chaplain, now Dean Hughes – to whom the west forecourt of the Cathedral was laid out as a memorial.

A little before that time, the Cathedral organist, Dr Moody, was having his own battle at the Cathedral. He disputed the Dean and Chapter's right to determine music for services and the Royal College of Organists took Moody's case to court. After learned discussion it was discovered that the case had been presented in the wrong court! An amicable compromise was reached and in 1945 Dr Moody hailed as … 'an historic chapter in the record of Cathedral music' the decision of the Dean and Chapter to revert to settings instead of chants, for the Sunday morning service.

Visitors sometimes ask if the Cathedral is 'High Church'? As mother church of the diocese, it presents a wide range of services. Vestments may or may not be worn and there may be music, processions or incense. The way that a particular service is presented will depend upon its purpose and upon the kind of congregation attending.

SOME MEMORABLE SERVICES

For many years the BBC has periodically broadcast Evensong from the Cathedral. One February, they were committed to recording on a specific day for later transmission. Unfortunately on the day set, there were particularly strong winds. It was almost impossible to open the doors against the wind and after the service, one of the basses remarked … 'I could hardly hear myself sing'. Unusually, the BBC had to apologise both before and after the recording for the remarkable sounds of the gale.

During the 1980's there were several televised productions and these invoked much heart-searching, and ask … 'does the enjoyment given to the many that do not, or cannot attend church, justify the massive (yes, massive) upheaval that is entailed'? In a Christmas broadcast in the late 1980's, viewers saw the Cathedral virtually as worshippers would see it on any day of the year – a notable achievement for TV in those days. But I recall one television production, when virtually everything that could be moved was moved; one felt that the immobility of the pulpit was almost resented. It is now several years since we had a 'TV Religious Spectacular' *(sighs of relief from the staff!).*

The church's year begins with Advent, which is marked at Ripon by a moving service of carols and readings. If it happens to be a year when one of the choristers has mastery of top C, Allegri's *Miserere* is an added joy of the evening. Just before Christmas, the boy and girl choristers, accompanied by a harpist, sing Benjamin Britten's *Ceremony of Carols* with the only light in the Cathedral that of the choristers' candles supplemented by a few on the platform. This is an occasion that is enhanced by subtracting light from the building, rather than adding it, using computer-controlled dimming (or raising) of the lighting. The same procedure is also used at the service of *Nine Lessons and Carols*, traditionally held on Christmas Eve, but now so popular that it has become necessary to duplicate it.

On Christmas Eve, we now have the *Journey to Bethlehem*, where Mums and Dads bring along their children, dressed as variously Joseph, Mary, shepherds or the innkeeper, and one of the clergy gives a dramatic running commentary on unfolding events. Christmas Eve 2009 was a dreadful day, yet the nave was packed. We are clearly getting on to the right wavelength!

A very popular introduction in recent years is the *Boxing Day Walk* from the Cathedral across the fields to Fountains Abbey, commemorating the monks' journey in 1132 (see Chapter 2). The hundreds who participate, join in a short act of worship in the Abbey.

At the *New Year's Eve service* which was introduced (or re-introduced) in 1985, the nave is tightly packed with people, both seated and standing. At the 1999/2000 service there was barely enough standing room in the nave and at one point in the service a wonderful, total stillness. After the service, the congregation streamed up to the Market Place (many of them carrying flaming torches, in those pre-Health & Safety days) where the Dean blessed the city from the Town Hall balcony. Older people greeted friends, while families took advantage of the unusually mild night to sit on the cobbles in the Market Place and enjoy a picnic.

Another notable event is the annual *St Wilfrid service*, which is held about the beginning of August to celebrate the return of St Wilfrid to Ripon long ago. For two hours on a Saturday afternoon, a rich assortment of bands, decorated floats and sometimes vintage cars processes around the city streets, with total paralysis of all through traffic. It starts at the Market Square which is tightly packed with people and where the first movement is by St Wilfrid himself, leaving the Town Hall on his white horse. One year, the long procession had barely started when several *cave men* leapt off the first float and kidnapped an attractive policewoman who was trying to control the traffic! After eventually making a comprehensive circuit of the town, everyone is back at the west front of the cathedral, and all the occupants of the floats wearing anything from grass skirts to ball gowns or monastic habits to football strip – not to mention wigs, beards, false noses and sundry balloons – pour off the vehicles into the Cathedral. A happy innovation in 2009 was that, for the first time, Ripon Cathedral had its own float, thanks to hard work by some young parents.

'St Wilfrid' himself on his white horse and clad in all the multi-layered finery of a bishop must suffer on hot days. A noble victim for the occasion, he always manages to look as though his entry into the Cathedral was yet another triumph.

Some readers will ask: '*What have events like this to do with a Cathedral?*' It should be appreciated that it is both parish church and Cathedral. The church, in general, should approach outsiders *where they are* and not from *where it is.* Moreover, in the Middle Ages, the Cathedral offered the only covered space where large events of any kind could occur. Of course the church's contacts with today's secular world could be better, but popular occasions like Harvest Festival or the St Wilfrid festival provide a starting point.

As in the Middle Ages, the church's year is punctuated by a series of services making full use of music, colour and processions.

New sets of vestments made by the Cathedral broderers in the 1970s add to the splendour of sung Eucharists, as also to the great occasions in the church's year: Candlemas, Holy Week, Easter, Pentecost, Ascensiontide, Christmas and ordinations. The Cathedral choir is usually on vacation when most people are having their annual summer holidays, potentially leaving gaps in the programme of sung services.

Gaps are often filled by visiting parish church choirs or by other groups of singers, who give anything from a day to a week of their own time to enrich the Cathedral's worship. Standards are high and it is interesting to hear new interpretations of works that are well established in the Cathedral's repertoire.

Ordination services (the ordination of priests and deacons) call for especial care, as we found one year when it had been decided to have the entire service video-filmed. The expert brought in for the occasion was shown where power points were and, more importantly, the total loading acceptable. At twenty minutes to zero the expert blew everything in the cathedral, the organ included, but luck was on our side: I managed to call in the cathedral electrician with only minutes to go. Never again has a service been video-filmed!

Since the summer of 2009, the 9.30 Eucharist on the first Sunday of the month has been enlivened by the new *Cathedral Music Group*. It can include a variety of instruments and there are singers and players of all ages. The emphasis is on simple tunes that are easy to sing so that the congregation can join in. A moving occasion in 2009 was the jazz eucharist one Saturday evening, with Duke Ellington's music and a packed nave. Almost everyone who attended received Holy Communion. The Holy Spirit is often thought of as:

'How silently, how silently the wondrous gift is given',

but Duke Ellington's music gave the feeling of a rushing mighty wind tearing through the building. For staid older people like the writer, it was a wonderful occasion.

Some years ago, the Cathedral's ten bells were in poor condition and enthusiasm for ringing had waned. Following a complete overhaul of the bells, and enhancing the number of them to 13, there is now an accomplished team of local people whose skills add to the enjoyment of special occasions.

OTHER EVENTS IN THE CATHEDRAL

Churches are now increasingly used for concerts, plays and other events. My experience as head verger was that those involving young people are sometimes both the most demanding and the most rewarding. In both 2009 and 2010, the cathedral linked up with teachers in the area and with Ballet Rambert, to give a moving dance production occupying most of the nave, and with a hundred young dancers. One delights in the considerable talent so often revealed and the unaffected competence of young participants.

Each Easter, groups of young people from all over the world converge on Harrogate for an International Youth Festival and the Cathedral is often the venue for some very gifted groups.

One recalls a German youth orchestra where four teenagers played a Bach fugue which they had arranged for brass; a Finnish youth choir with immense mastery over a range extending from Palestrina to contemporary Scandinavian music and a Lithuanian choir singing a remarkable modern work, *Approaching storm and Aurora Borealis* which presented every sound from the first sighing of wind in grass to the fusillade of raindrops on foliage and the crash of thunder. This was modern music at its best, in a performance that left no doubt as to the talents of conductor and choir. The concert was given shortly before the collapse of Communism in Eastern Europe and ended poignantly with the *Hymn of Freedom*.

A chance encounter some years ago with the headmaster of a large Roman Catholic comprehensive school in the north-east led, for many years, to their school band, orchestra and choir holding its annual concert in the Cathedral. The director of music was a former RAF bandmaster and his programmes included everything from simple arrangements of the classics to entire movements of concertos or a stunning big band sound. The choir was equally 'catholic' in taste and one hopes that many youngsters will retain memories of exercising their skills in this fine setting. My wife and I enjoyed the privilege of sitting in the front row, with the headmaster and his wife.

Drama is more difficult to present because of the Cathedral's acoustic eccentricities, which can tax even accomplished companies. Nevertheless, a youth company from Somerset gave in the 1980's an unforgettable performance of *Godspell*. In the final act, the crucifixion, one felt that the group had transcended mere acting. At rehearsal, I (unwisely) sat at the front of the nave and received a smacking red kiss from one of the 'naughty ladies'. Thirty years on, the producer and I still exchange Christmas cards.

Soldiers of the Royal Engineers based at Ripon have the freedom of the City of Ripon. Each year, detachments attend Cathedral services to the great pleasure of onlookers who watch the immaculate lines of marchers with – as their 'freedom' allows – bayonets fixed. The sound of the regimental band seated below the centre tower and playing Elgar's *Nimrod* is not soon forgotten, nor is that of a Gurkha company playing their bagpipes on another occasion. Some years ago, when heating in the church was rudimentary, an American contingent was on parade in February and had to suffer an hour's immobility in church, clad in their lightweight uniforms: best not to ask what their recollections of the occasion are.

An especially moving service was the funeral of the Royal Engineers' adjutant, an occasion marked by the immaculate turn out of the troops and their total precision. The coffin, draped with the Union Jack, bore the adjutant's hat and sword. Relationships between garrison and city are cordial and the city is indebted to the Royal Engineers for many acts of goodwill.

For many years the church has been loyally served by a band of voluntary guides who are there to answer visitors' questions or to show parties around. Then a successful 'Ministry of Welcome' was introduced, with voluntary helpers greeting visitors on arrival and helping to make them feel at home, and we now have the first voluntary chaplains on duty, too. Free leaflets are available in many languages but inevitably in such a small community (Ripon's population is nearing 17,000) few of the helpers can speak a foreign language. I asked one man which language he would like. 'Latvian', he replied. 'Would Russian do?', I asked. 'Fine' he answered! My small repertoire includes phrases in Welsh, German and Polish, but I can say from experience that for those making the effort, the fact that they did try compensates for linguistic shortcomings. It was a guide from Coventry Cathedral, years ago, who remarked that visitors will forget what was said, but not the person who said it.

In a Cathedral town, some polarisation between church and town is inevitable. At Ripon, a notable joining of the two was achieved at a *Ripon Today* week in 1986, when the whole of the nave was filled with stalls and demonstrations by most of the organisations in town, including Morris dancing, flower arrangements and karate, and the church was alive with local people learning about local activities and making new friends in the process.

Happily, events like that are no longer a rarity. In recent years there have been well-attended events appealing to families, such as combats on the forecourt between well-protected men wielding swords, battleaxes or lances! There are days, too, when the whole nave is given over to children's crafts and skills. In the Middle Ages the church was the only possible venue for so many activities and, happily, history is repeating itself. It all began with Dean Edwin le Grice ordering portable staging and stacking chairs, over thirty years ago.

One of the Cathedral's finest moments in recent years was the Royal Maundy, in 1985. On Maundy Thursday, 4th April, 1985, a huge procession was lined up at the west end of the nave, facing the great west doors. For some minutes the only sound was the murmur of the waiting crowd outside, until it rose to a crescendo: the Queen's car was coming up Bedern Bank!

For the Cathedral staff it was the culmination of many months of careful planning. Immense care was taken in preparing the list of people to whom tickets would be granted and this occupied most of two people's time for several weeks.

An exact floor plan of the church was needed to determine the location of every numbered seat. Then schedules were prepared of the arrivals of all dignitaries and where they would park their cars. A list was needed too, of all who would assemble in the Dean's house after the service, with a chance of meeting the Queen and the Duke of Edinburgh.

Just before the day itself, there was a full rehearsal of all who would be involved, with stand-ins for the Queen and the Duke. Imagine our horror when a local taximan's voice suddenly boomed over the Cathedral's loudspeakers (radio microphones were in use at the time). Over the years, different kinds of radio microphone, mixer and amplifier have been used, and the microphones in those days frequently topped the list of complaints from the congregation. There were no problems at the Maundy Service itself.

At the Royal Maundy rehearsal, recipients were warned by a senior police officer on no account to succumb to dealers hovering around after the service. 'If anyone approaches you', he said, 'yell "Mike" at the top of your voice, and I'll sort it out. Keep your Maundy money in a safe place'. Staff members were each given a token set of coins and to my family's disgust, the writer's money is safe today, in a casket placed on top of the obelisk in the Market Place.

The day before the Maundy service, a coach arrived bringing the *Yeomen of the Guard* and other officials. It was my privilege to receive the immense gold plates dating from the time of Charles II, which would be used to hold the Maundy money. Plates and money were put away safely for the night. Each recipient gets two bags of money, one is for 'expenses' and the other holds silver pennies, equal in number to the years of the sovereigns age.

(It was a humbling experience, the day before the event, to meet the Yeomen and learn their single job responsibility – to defend the life of the sovereign, at whatever cost).

The day itself began, for me, in an unexpected way. The previous night, I had handed the cathedral keys to a senior army officer before going home, keeping just the keys needed to enter next day. It was dark when I entered next morning and I called out … 'Is anyone there?' No reply, to my surprise. I walked to the west end and there stood the biggest dog I've ever seen in my life. 'You've had a long night', I said nonchalantly to it. I walked to the west door and unlocked it. A soldier standing there looked at me, his expression aghast. 'Didn't he get you'?, he said.

After the Queen, the Duke of Edinburgh and all dignitaries had been met at the west door, they were conducted to the high altar, passing on the way the Yeomen of the Guard who stood to attention holding their *trainers*, or pikes. After the procession came two Yeomen, each bearing over his head a plate heaped up with the bags of money.

These they carried into the choir at the east end and slowly lowered them – with straight backs, no pursuit for anyone with lumbago – on to a waist-high table. At a previous Maundy service, we learned, one of the two Yeomen had realised on entering the Cathedral that his new hat was slowly slipping over his eyes! He followed closely behind his colleague and just managed to keep his heels in sight, until he reached the table for depositing the money.

One big task shortly to be tackled, is the complete overhaul of the organ. A costly matter, but the kind of project that, the longer it is deferred, the greater the final cost will be. Ripon's musical reputation is substantial and only the best is good enough!

Another substantial project in the offing is to be the construction of a glass entrance, or narthex, to replace the very unwelcoming Victorian entrance porch at the west end; a project having the financial support of a local business man.

One local lady determined upon a spectacular celebration of the millenium. *Connie Birkinshaw* resolved that embroidered cushions should be placed all along the stone benches, against the outside walls of the nave. She recruited 12 teams of people, drawn from far and wide, firstly to design and then to execute the work, which illustrates on one side of the nave the town's history, and on the other the sights of the city today. The cushions are said to contain over two million stitches. Fine new cushions were also made for the steps to the high altar and for the new Chapel of Justice and Peace at the west end of the north nave aisle.

The word 'million' reminds me of the moving 'Six Million Buttons' exhibition here in 2010. Initiated by churches in Leeds, this was a travelling exhibition, with each button standing for someone killed in the Holocaust in World War Two and in other barbarous spells of modern history.

At the exhibition, I spoke with a man who had survived internment at Auschwitz .

SO MUCH FOR HISTORY ... ...

Ripon Cathedral gives much thought to visitors, to visitor/heritage considerations, to worship and to money, in an age which is ever more concerned with leisure and tourism. In ending our section on the Cathedral's history, one wonders what challenges it will face in the future.

Part 2: Chapters 9 - 20

ARCHITECTURE

THE CATHEDRAL AND ITS CONTENTS

Figure 9: summarising the main periods of construction and the ages and styles of parts of the Cathedral standing today (not to scale).

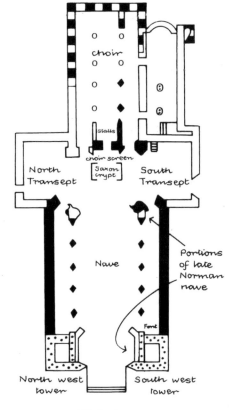

Saxon crypt below
centre tower
Transitional Norman c.1184
Early English c.1220
Decorated c. 1300
Perpendicular c. 1500

Century	Style	Disaster	Building / rebuilding
7	[ ] Saxon		(Crypt survives)
10		Destroyed by fire.	Rebuilt, but details are unknown.
11-12	?		Assorted stones remain.
12-13	Late Norman		Choir, centre tower, transepts, nave (without aisles.) chapter house.
13	Early English		West front added.
13		East end fell	
14	Decorated		New east end
14	Perpendicular		Lady chapel added above chapter house.
15	Perpendicular	Parts of centre tower, choir, south transept fell, and	... were rebuilt. Choir stalls carved.
16	Perpendicular	South and north walls of nave fell	Nave rebuilt with addition of aisles.
17		Fall of spire on centre tower. Spires on west end removed.	Spires never replaced.

CHAPTER 9

The Saxon church

WHEN ST WILFRID WENT TO ROME in the mid-seventh century, its fine stone buildings must have greatly impressed him after Northumbria's timber and thatch.

Many Roman churches were basilicas (modelled upon the law courts and public assembly halls of the day), a fact that influenced James Ashworth's drawing (Fig. 10). But Wilfrid could equally have copied other styles, seen by him in either Rome or Canterbury. His biographer, Eddius, is not helpful over detail and apart from the crypt, tangible evidence at Ripon is meagre.

St. Peter's, Ripon, 672 - 950

Figure 10

Drawing by James Ashworth

Whatever the style, the building of a stone church would have called for craft skills not seen in Northumbria since Roman times and Wilfrid must have compiled a list of his needs, somewhat as follows:-

Stonemasons...

... able to identify likely sources of stone, preferably not far from the building site, with knowledge of building techniques used in Rome, including using mortar and plaster

... able to survey and level the site for building and -

Blacksmiths...

... able to make and maintain all the tools used by the masons and carpenters,

... able to make iron fastenings of various kinds. It is not known from where the iron was obtained (Colsterdale was a source in later centuries, when it is known that iron was being made at Fountains Abbey) but the blacksmith was the number one craftsman: no blacksmith, no tools.

Carpenters...

... able to erect scaffolding and build the timber formers upon which stones would be assembled for windows, arches and vaults.

Plumbers and glaziers...

Eddius recorded how Wilfrid had the church at York repaired in 670, just two years before the consecration of his own church in Ripon. Plumbers repaired the leaky roof (probably with lead from Nidderdale) and glass was put in the windows through which birds were flying, 'so as to admit light but not rain'. So it is likely that glass windows were installed at Ripon: the manufacture of glass in Saxon Northumbria is well authenticated, and it must have been some of the earliest glass in England.

Some at least of the craftsmen needed to build the Saxon church (artist's impression in Figure 10) would have been brought by Wilfrid from Rome, for all building in England at that time was in wood, like the royal palaces at Yeavering and Cheddar.

Wilfrid's church is long gone but the crypt has survived and could be the earliest complete church structure of stone in England. It is also, along with Hexham – built soon afterwards – of a design unique in Western Europe. Furthermore, the measurements of the two crypts are in multiples of one-third of a northern rod of 16.5 feet and the widths of the two main chambers are identical (Bailey).

The crypt entrance today (Fig. 11) is down steps from the nave but in St Wilfrid's day, it was near the big archway through the stone screen.

Why the change? Wilfrid's crypt was unaltered for half a millenium until the central tower of Archbishop Roger's church was erected above it and access to pilgrims could no longer be down the original north passage.

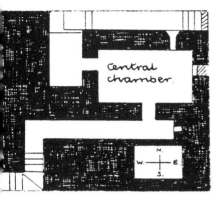

Figure 11: plan of the crypt and access passages as they are today

Subsequently (until the 1970s), the only entrance to the crypt was from the south side. One is so absorbed by taking this step back in time as to be oblivious of the very botched appearance of the stonework. The entrance was probably created in the early sixteenth century when work on the tower was ending and creation of the new nave south aisle was about to begin. The masons were too concerned with making something new to bother overmuch about what had gone before!

One then turns right into the south passage of the crypt. Overhead are two roof stones, one with a large cross and its neighbour with circles and lines. At the top of the wall, nearby, there are on the north side two mason's marks on stones that are well-dressed and obviously later than adjoining masonry. Here, we meet the first of a number of light recesses in the crypt walls. The main chamber (Photo 1, p.169) has five of these recesses or *cressets*, one still with the hollow in the base for holding oil and a wick. All but one of the others were filled with cement in modern times by a tidy-minded mason! The large recess on the east wall probably contained something of great value: a crucifix or a relic, perhaps.

The upper surface of the chamber's barrel roof was first recorded in detail in the early 1930's and seen by a fortunate few, including the writer, in the 1980's.

Until 1975, the north passage ended at a steep, but blocked, flight of steps leading towards a little chamber within the pulpitum (the stone screen separating choir and nave), which is where the winding wooden stair was then inserted. Five years earlier and at the west end of the passage, it had been observed that one of the steps bore signs of carving and it was carefully removed. Later put in the treasury (Fig. 12), it bears a braided pattern similar to that on other stones at Saxon sites in the north-east and may be re-used Roman material from nearby Aldborough (Bailey).

So much for the crypt's structure today. What we should like to know is why was it built? What was it used for? What changes were later made to it and why?

Figure 12

Carved patterns of Italian design adorn this re-used Roman stone.

Was it built primarily to hold relics? Certainly, they were needed for the consecration of new churches and relics brought pilgrims - and their offerings. In early churches, the altar held either the body of the saint to whom the church was dedicated, or else a relic associated with him and Wilfrid's church, being among the first in England to become a cathedral, would naturally be appealed to as a source of relics.

One more problem remains: where did the townsfolk worship? It is unlikely that they would have been allowed in the church containing the crypt, if it was indeed the 'conventual church', i.e. the church of the monastery (Walbran thought that it was not). Did they use the Ladykirk, excavated in modern times just to the north-east of the Old Deanery? And although Ripon did have a parish church of Allhallows in the Middle Ages, our knowledge of it is confined to Leland's reference, centuries later, to its ruinous state.

When Eadred set the church on fire in 950 with a view to destroying it, the crypt survived and may have played a part in the discreditable veneration of relics that developed in succeeding centuries. There is a late medieval reference to 'paying two clerks to wash the relics' and at York, the occasion had the status of a festival.

In Elizabeth I's reign, Thomas Blackburn was ordered to … 'stop up the place within the church called St Wilfrid's needle' and to take down the altar that stood there (the needle was the former light recess that now communicates with the north passage). In the following centuries both Camden and John Ray referred – perhaps tongue-in-cheek – to ladies determining their chastity according to whether they could 'thread the needle'. Indeed, ladies enjoyed this pursuit up to the end of the 19th century, with the vergers sometimes helping them towards a favourable diagnosis.

Investigations within the last hundred years, professional and amateur, have revealed deposits of both human and animal bones, under the floor and within the walls; perhaps they were relics, hidden at the Reformation. One 19th-century investigator was the canons' verger, described by an admiring contemporary as having 'considerable experience in these matters'.

An outstanding exhibit today in the cathedral treasury, is the circular piece of Saxon jewellery. Discovered by archaeologists in 1978, it was just a few paces from the writer's raspberry bed and presented to the cathedral on loan. Its gold framework contains amethysts and garnets and it dates from about the time of St Wilfrid. Was it perhaps attached to the cover of a book? Even, remote possibility, to the Gospels that St Wilfrid himself gave to the new church for its consecration?

CHAPTER 10

The missing years
(c. 950-1180)

TO ANTIQUARIANS, A SINGLE CARVED STONE – or even part of one – can open up a new chapter about the church and it is regrettable how many ancient stones have been lost here over the years.

When Leland was here in Henry VIII's time, he observed 'three very old crosses' by the Ladykirk. Whether or not they were Saxon, is not known. But we do know that in the mid-19th century, a 'portion of a Saxon grave cross' was found in the Deanery Garden (close by the site of the Ladykirk) and given to the York Museum; it bore the inscription † ADHUSE (P) RB (Fowler). In 1832 another cross had been dug up in the churchyard and placed over the undercroft door (Walbran), but it was given away a century or more later!

In the middle of the twentieth century, alterations in the Chapter House revealed some old stones: two went to Ripon, Wisconsin but the fate of the others is not known. At about this time, Canon Bartlett described a cylindrical column fragment found south of Priest Lane. Maybe it is the piece (sandstone, of diameter no more than four inches) which until 1990 was in the garden of Old Deanery Cottage but has since been lost.

The late Norman builders were more particular about such objects and the two carved stones on the outside of the north transept (Fig. 13) have survived perhaps 1,000 years to intrigue amateurs and experts alike.

Turning now to relics that have not been jettisoned, a notable discovery occurred in 1975 when alterations were being made to the Markenfield Chapel. The Sigurd stone found there and carved in the days of the Viking kingdom of Yorvik, combines Christian tradition with Viking mythology as Sigurd, on one side of the cross fragment, sucks his thumb after slaying Fafnir the dragon. Lang described the stone as being similar to another, once in the crypt but no longer in the cathedral.

Two irregularly cut sandstone column bases, of a design quite unlike anything to be seen in the cathedral, were until 1992 in a nearby garden but have now been moved into the church. Richard Bailey and Richard Hall date them as 11th or 12th century.

Figure 13

Saxon stones built into the 12th century exterior wall of the North Transept. Their patterns resemble the knots of ancient crosses.

Today, only the Chapter House undercroft contains any significant amount of masonry dating from before Roger's time, apart from the crypt.

The most significant archaeological find of recent decades was in 1932 when the floor below the centre tower was taken up. Parallel with the crypt's north and south passages nearby, were foundations of two walls, evidently belonging to an earlier church. At the west end of each wall (and close to the two western piers of the centre tower) was a substantial 'drum stone'. That on the north side, of gritstone and 3ft 6in diameter, now stands in the undercroft where it has been inverted to serve as an altar. A circular scar on the smaller flat face (no longer visible) shows that it was almost certainly a column base (Hall). The other drum was left *in situ* and is, curiously, of different material and diameter: limestone, 3ft 10in. I am not aware of precise dates having been assigned to either the walls or the drums.

The church's negligent attitude in the past towards objects of 'architectural, archaeological, artistic or historic interest' is now at an end, thanks to recent legislation. The new *Care of Cathedrals Measure* requires cathedrals to prepare and maintain an inventory of all such objects and 'no loan, sale or other disposal' may be made without the authority of the Cathedrals Fabric Council, itself empowered by Statutory Instrument 1990 No 2335: that is indeed good news and such an account was compiled a few years ago by Mrs Diana Balmforth.

CHAPTER 11

Archbishops Roger and De Grey
and a diagnosis of
the masons' troubles

INTRODUCTION

How many English cathedrals can rival ours in its history of structural disasters? There have been so many changes to the original structure since building began in the late 12th century that this introduction will, I hope, make matters easier to understand.

Much of the church we see today was begun by Archbishop Roger around 1180 in a late Norman style (with round and pointed arches: pointed arches were the very latest discovery) and the west front was finished early in the following century by Archbishop Walter de Grey in a totally new style.

Over the centuries there have been several structural disasters, usually followed by rebuilding in the latest style. What were the causes?

TWELFTH CENTURY PROBLEMS

Work in the late C12 got off to a poor start, for the centre tower began to lean north-westwards as it was being built. In the following centuries, trouble arose with successively the east end of the church, the centre tower and parts of the choir south aisle and the south transept, the side walls of the nave and finally - in Victorian times - the west front!

The principal cause of trouble was that the church was built in the wrong place. Wilfrid was one of the greatest churchmen to date in England and it was natural to rebuild on the site of his church (consecrated in 672); in fact the centre tower of Roger's church was exactly above St Wilfrid's crypt. St Wilfrid's church was small, it lacked the lofty eminence of later Roman and Gothic churches and above all, it barely extended eastwards on to the sloping, sandy terrain used later for Roger's church: a disastrous combination for a new church of such height as Roger's.

Other factors contributing to successive troubles over the years were:

- The church's **foundations** were inadequate, but few churches in previous centuries had ever been built on this scale. When in the 1970s work was being done in the north transept chapel, I saw how shallow the foundations were. That had already been learned in Victorian times when the fabric of the west front was at risk and Sir George Gilbert Scott was engaged to make new foundations beneath the west front of the church.

- The master mason had aspired to the loftiness of later Gothic churches but his **rubble-filled walls** were potentially weak - and early buttresses were notably more aesthetic than functional. Look at the outside wall of the Choir on the north side, next to the transept and compare with the later, adjacent buttresses to the east.

- It was not realised how great the **wind force** can be on a high building. One day in the 80s, the BBC was broadcasting choral evensong from the Cathedral. The noise of the wind at the time was so tumultuous that apologies were made to listeners about it. As I stood under the centre tower during the broadcast, I could feel through my shoes the vibrations of the wind on the fabric: my only such experience in fifteen years at the cathedral. I hope it never happens again.

- Nor was it appreciated that the **wider the building** (and many English Cathedrals are less wide than Ripon), the greater the **outward thrust** of the roof on the outer walls. The unusually wide nave had no side aisles, which would have acted as three-dimensional buttresses - so its days were numbered.

- **Fashion**, or rivalry between one master mason and another, became increasingly significant in church design and this led to enthusiasm outstripping the master masons' knowledge of building structures: they unwittingly created problems never before imagined. To adapt a popular song of years ago, 'Anything you can build I can build bigger, I can build anything bigger than you'. Ken Follett handled this dramatically in his novel "Pillars of the Earth". Roger's master mason for example was either ignorant of the *tetrapylon* structure needed to support centre towers, or he ignored it: (refer to Hugh Braun's book, *Cathedral Architecture*). So the tower began to lean as it was being built and the evidence is there today for one to see, several centuries later.

Chronologically, this is how events developed:

- **Marking out the ground** probably began at what is now the north-west corner of the north transept (Harrison).

- As work began on the centre tower it was **only supported adequately under its two eastern corners** and the north-east corner began to lean north-westwards.

The adjoining arches in the north transept and the choir became distorted (the evidence is still there to see) and the arch leading from the north transept to the choir north aisle had to be filled in. Just inside the choir north aisle one can see the clever improvisation adopted to stabilise the structure. The problem was so serious that the tower was never built to its originally intended height, as Harrison and Barker proved by careful measurements of the exterior.

- Before the nave had been completed to the west end, **the original plans of Archbishop Roger were completely changed by Archbishop de Grey.** Instead of ending in a simple gable – as originally planned - the west front was built with three tiers of windows and twin flanking towers. But the new design meant that the west end was much higher than originally planned, so the nave walls had to be raised, and also, in turn, those of the transepts!

- Within decades of the west front's completion, **serious problems had developed at the east end** (on its sandy site), necessitating substantial rebuilding. The east front and some easternmost bays were remodelled with massive buttresses outside replacing the slender twelfth century ones: study at ground level outside the north-east angle of the central tower to see how masons became more aware of the problems arising with such big buildings. Flying buttresses, which begin not at ground level but higher up, came into use.

- A century and a half passed then an **earth tremor**, it's said (and Ripon, which is in a gypsum-subsidence area, has had a tremor in modern times, causing every note of my piano to go out of tune!) - caused the centre tower to partially collapse. But the building was on **sandy terrain** anyway, and there was no understanding in the twelfth century of the importance of **buttressing**.

- The coup de grace came in the early sixteenth century when the south and north **sides of the nave successively fell**. The only surprise is that they had survived for so long, without side aisles which would have supported them.

- By 1546 most of the Minster's **revenues had been seized** by Henry VIII and the centre tower has remained in its unfinished state ever since.

- In the seventeenth century, the **centre tower spire crashed down** and it was deemed wise to remove the spires at the west end too.

- But that was not an end to the Minster's troubles. By the mid-nineteenth century **cracks had developed in the west front,** big enough to take a man's hand, and the Victorian architect Sir George Gilbert Scott was engaged to rectify matters. He found that inside the south-west tower interments had occurred to a greater depth than the foundations and he had to create **new foundations** beneath the thirteenth century masonry.

Massive balks of timber were used to shore up the west front in stages while new masonry was placed beneath the original stonework. The last step was to burn away the final balk of timber after soaking it in oil, leaving the west front fully supported on the new masonry. Apparently, the locals were sure the whole west front would collapse and gathered, at a respectable distance in Bedern Bank, in happy anticipation of the worst (I was given this story by an elderly friend, who heard it in his youth from an old Riponian).

Despite all vicissitudes, much of Archbishop Roger's church has lasted over 800 years. The design of Wilfrid's church embodied well-tried Roman building techniques, whereas Archbishop Roger's church could be described as *a conflict between untested technology and unsuitable terrain.*

To take the latter point first: Roger had almost limitless level ground available to the west of the present site, so why did he head for trouble by reaching eastwards on to a sloping, sandy site? The answer is the presence of the Saxon crypt, which was to be as essential a feature of Roger's church as it had been of Wilfrid's. By the 12th century however the size of churches had increased greatly and it is also likely that Wilfrid's church terminated not far east of the crypt, so Roger was obliged to build on ground which Wilfrid had wisely avoided.

Now taking the point of untested technology: the largest feature of a Gothic cathedral in terms of area is the nave, but in the Byzantine churches of Roger's day, most of the floor space lay beneath the dome, which was supported on four structures rather like square stools *(tetrapylons),* with round arches between the legs instead of rectangular spaces. The stools projected just far enough beyond the dome to constitute embryonic arms. Imagine now the dome replaced by a tower and the arms lengthened: the result is a cruciform church with a centre tower (Hugh Braun).

Roger's church first developed structural problems at a very early date. Harrison and Barker have reasoned that the centre tower was either not built to the originally intended height, or was actually lowered. Serious movement of the fabric certainly occurred at the north-east angle of the tower. The evidence for that is the serious cracks and displacement of fabric, clearly visible in the central tower viewed from north transept. It would have been at that time that the archway leading into the choir north aisle had to be filled-in, with strengthening ribs inserted behind it – a simple and effective device that has withstood the passage of many centuries (Photos 4 and 5, p.170),

The nave

A practical question: how did the masons control the heights of the successive storeys, as they built? The answer is that on reaching the desired height for the first storey, they laid a shallow course of flat stone - a string course - often slightly projecting. On that, they placed their storey rods to check the height of the next storey.

Looking at that feature of the nave one day, I was reminded of early schooldays and learning *Tables*: the last line of one table went, "5-and-a-half yards make one rod, pole or perch". The masons had gone to lunch so (in pre-Health and Safety days) I borrowed a ladder, got someone to foot it and ascended with a tape measure. The height of the next storey? – sure enough, $5^1/_2$ yards. How meaningless it was at school - but here was the explanation.

From a quick glance at the nave one might think that little of Roger's work has survived and certainly not enough to reconstruct its original appearance. James Ashworth's reconstruction well captures the feel of Roger's nave (Fig. 14) but his interpretation of surviving Roger-fabric was incorrect. Note though, the impressive rood beam with its figures of Mary, Christ and St John that formerly occupied the rebates (still visible) at each side of the tower arch.

Harrison and Barker have measured and recorded every surviving detail of Roger's fabric, and Harrison's reconstruction of the nave appears in Fig. 15.

Before glass was available, early buildings had to make do with shutters, or removable frames covered with oiled cloth. As late as the fourteenth century; the minster accounts mention … 'repairs to the fixed windows', but perhaps that was exceptional. In any case, had the structure been pierced by additional windows, without the support of aisles, it would have been intolerably weakened.

Figure 14: James Ashworth's reconstruction of Roger's nave

Only fragments of the nave, at the west and east ends, survived the fall of the side walls in the early sixteenth century. The walls of the west towers facing into the nave are of Transitional Norman style, whereas the other side is in Early English! This becomes clear if one stands inside the south-west tower and looks across to the nave wall on the north side. The change from one style to another was not easy: other imperfections of detail reveal the difficulties arising in joining de Grey's west front to Roger's nave. On the south side for example, the head of the new pointed arch is markedly off-centre whilst on the north side, the rising shafts in the corner are not vertical. Also, although hardly visible from

Archbishop Roger's nave : Stuart Harrison's reconstruction.

Bays 10 and 11 not shown.

Figure 15

the ground, high on the north side, old masonry of Roger's fabric has been dressed off quite crudely to accommodate the new west front. Finally, in the north clerestory, there is a neat rectangular gap where the string course formerly ran further westwards (Fig. 16). Notice too the straight joints at the top of the wall where there were formerly roof timbers. Finally, note that the gap from west to east between Roger's nave and the later sixteenth century rebuilding is much wider on the south side than on the north!

But de Grey's stonemasons had to cope with much more complex matters than off-centre arches or non-vertical shafts. Quite simply, the new west front was too high for Roger's nave.

Looking at the west end of the nave north wall (Fig. 17), shafts now run up to a string course and no longer support the roof above. Indeed, on the other (north) side of the wall, inside the north-west tower (Fig. 18), there is a *corbel table* (a slightly projecting ledge of stone, supported on projecting blocks, or *corbels*) obviously put there to support the nave roof just as the similar corbel tables in Roger's choir and north transept did (Fig. 19).

Figure 16: missing link

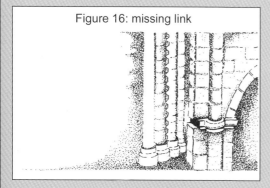

Figure 17: west end of north nave wall

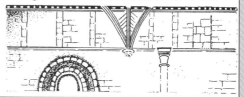

Figure 18: corbel table inside N.W. tower

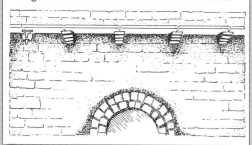

Figure 19

Figure 20

Figure 21: types of buttress

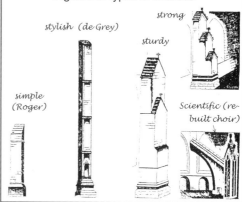

stylish (de Grey)

strong

sturdy

simple (Roger)

Scientific (re-built choir)

Figure 22

A century or more before Agincourt

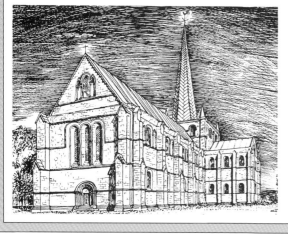

Exterior of Ripon Minster c. 1180-1450 (Archbishop Roger's building). The two west towers were added by Archbishop de Grey in the early thirteenth century, together with the whole west front.

Now consider what happened when the raised nave wall met the north transept (Fig. 20. The nave wall today is of course post-de Grey, but of similar height. The nave wall was so much higher than the transept wall that the latter had to be raised by several feet and the rain water discharge from the nave is higher than that from the north transept, which in turn is higher than that from the choir (see Fig. 19). It was fortunate that the west towers were added to Roger's church, because without them, the nave wall would never have withstood the battering to which the wind subjects the fabric with a force proportional to the square of the wind speed. Not only were there no aisles to support the nave, but Roger's slender buttresses were more decorative than useful and not to be compared with the massive buttresses built later in the church's history (Figure 21).

The depth of the nave's foundations is not known, but when Gilbert Scott was engaged in 1861 to avert what appeared to be the imminent collapse of the west front, his masons had to create new foundations, reaching 12 to 14 feet below those of de Grey.

So the nave somehow survived for three centuries, but the choir's survival was to prove much shorter. Ideas on building were changing rapidly. Roger's masons had enjoyed bringing round and pointed arches together in varying combinations; but there was little decorative work. Whether Roger's nave was ever finished is not known but, if it was, Fig. 22 shows how the west end would probably have looked.

De Grey's men produced a totally different kind of elevation, with row upon row of slim, pointed arches, liberally decorated with either nail-head or dog-tooth ornament (Fig. 23). Originally three tiers of windows opened into the nave but with later changes to the roof, the top tier was effectively lost (compare Photo 12, p.171 with the inside back cover): it now merely lights a passage going across the west gable.

The inspiration for the new style of the west front must have come from the continent, for there is a strong hint of *continental west work* (Hugh Braun), with porches surmounting an upper room.

Ripon's west front is widely acknowledged to be one of the finest English examples of this style of architecture (Front cover).

THE NORTH TRANSEPT

This is the finest surviving work of Roger's building. It is instructive to stand, first, in the churchyard facing the south door Figure 24). Note the rugged mass of the *south transept*, little removed in style from that of a Norman castle. Now step inside and look towards the opposite, north transept (Figures 25, 26).

Figure 23

Dog tooth   Nail head

The north wall is notable for its lack of symmetry, its galleries, plate tracery and its wonderful synthesis of round and pointed arches (Photo 7, p.170).

A closer look reveals that the bay widths vary. In the south transept they are symmetrical but not so in the north transept, where the triforium arches show a pleasing lack of symmetry, and good examples of plate tracery.

In the floor, at the foot of the north wall of the north transept is perhaps the oldest grave slab in the church, with its much-worn cross at one end.

At an early date, the Markenfield Chapel had a partition coming forward from the east wall, as the present scar testifies. A well-made *piscina* to the right (a recess in the wall with a drain hole for pouring away the rinsings from a chalice) is perhaps not original. On the north wall is a cupboard that has been crudely inserted to reveal the wall's rubble infill behind.

Above the chapel itself is the finest *vaulting* (i.e. arched roofing) in the cathedral (Fig. 27). It is hard to believe that there was a serious proposal only a few years ago to plaster it over! Vaults like this were never easy to construct and it could be a blessing, in limestone districts, to have a fairly soft stone available that presented fewer demands in achieving a good fit: the cutting of hard sandstone blocks left little margin for error.

Possibly, the masons made a trial assembly of the vault at ground level to confirm the *goodness of fit*. The final stone was the keystone at the top, which was lowered into place using a hook fitting into a recess at the top of the stone: a *Lewis*. Until a few years ago, there was such a stone lying on the ground at Fountains Abbey.

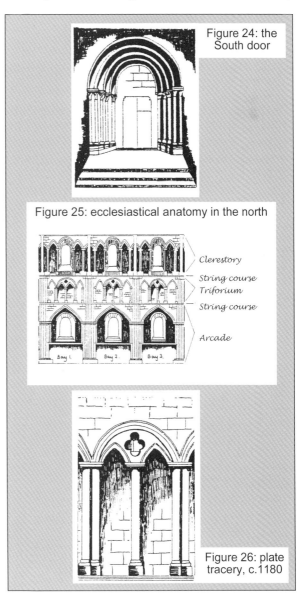

Figure 24: the South door

Figure 25: ecclesiastical anatomy in the north

Clerestory

String course
Triforium

String course

Arcade

Bay 1.   Bay 2.   Bay 3.

Figure 26: plate tracery, c.1180

Figure 27

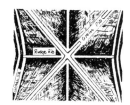

The roof of the Markenfield Chapel.

Also evident on the wall are remains of geometric patterns, painted with a dark pigment and possibly going back to Roger's period (there are similar vestiges in the south transept). In the chapel, there is an unusual example of a stone bearing *two* masons' marks: probably one from the mason at the quarry and the other for the mason fitting it in the cathedral.

THE CENTRAL TOWER

At many churches around this time, towers collapsed because the craftsmen's skill fell short of their enthusiasm. Beverley was typical: a priest rang the bell for morning service and just after his brethren reached the church, down came the tower. Crossley refers in *The English Abbey* to *the downfall of insecurely built towers*. It was not realised at Ripon in the twelfth century that round arches are inherently weaker than pointed ones. To add to the confusion, Pevsner points out that the north-west corner of the tower is asymmetrically sited in the wrong place!

The surviving late Norman walls appear externally to present their original window frames but even a casual glance at the passage walls high up inside the tower, with their many *straight joints* (masonry that is not bonded-in horizontally) gives evidence of later changes. An odd feature of the tower is that its ceiling is not rectangular, due to the position of the north-west corner.

The high cylindrical column rising from the floor by the tower's north-west pier, now crowned by James I, looks like an afterthought. Perhaps there were originally two columns, at the north-west and south-west corners, bearing statues of St Peter and St Wilfrid?

It is not known when a spire was first placed on the tower, but did the massive stones (corbels) that project inwards, high up on the west wall, once help to support a spire? It is hard to imagine what other purpose they might have had.

In the year 1227, Henry III gave 30 trees (20 rafters and 10 beams) for work on the tower, from the royal forest of Oakden. Since the west front of the church is associated with Archbishop de Grey (1216-1255), this suggests that work could have been proceeding simultaneously on both the centre tower and the west front – with its twin towers.

Tower cornice   Figure 28

It is noticeable that all three towers have similar cornices (Barker; Fig. 28): the cornice is the decorative band of stonework at the top of the tower wall.

SOUTH TRANSEPT

Did Roger's church have a *Lady Chapel* in the south transept? In considering the possibility, it is appropriate to bear contemporary church history in mind. The Cistercian *Abbey of St Mary of the Springs* (Fountains Abbey) was established three miles from Ripon in the early twelfth century by former Benedictine monks from St Mary's of York. Byland Abbey, also Cistercian and also dedicated to St Mary, dates from the same period. Ripon Minster was already dedicated to St Peter but it would be considered desirable (perhaps essential?) to have a chapel dedicated to Our Lady.

Significantly, the east wall of the south transept contains two well made cupboards, almost certainly of Roger's period and on the south wall is a notable piscina, which was partially wrecked (!) when the Aislabie memorial was created. Nearby, too, is the fine medieval wall painting of the Virgin and child, a supplicant and a figure with a scourge. There, surely, was the first Lady Chapel. The wall supporting the painting was built later than the choir south aisle, as the straight joint a little west of the Chapter House door (behind the organ pipes) testifies. Hallett thought that the first Lady Chapel was in the Chapter House apse, with its old cupboard and piscina to either side but more probably the chapel was moved there when the Ladyloft was built in the fourteenth century.

It would have been realised at an early date that the east end of the choir – the usual location for a Lady Chapel – was unsuitable because of the sloping site and in any case, we know that the shrine of St Wilfrid was behind the high altar at an early date.

THE CHOIR

Roger's choir was of six bays, as now, and the easternmost pillar on each side is original and probably in its original place.

But on the north side, the second and third pillars from the east now converge towards the central axis of the choir. After the east end of the choir fell, the pillars had been rebuilt and the wall above the arcade was thickened. The three heads above the third pillar from the east end date from that time (Photo 8, p.171). The face looking east has a respectable demeanour, but not so that facing across the choir. The uppermost (*clerestory*) level of the choir on the north side and the first three bays east of the tower appear at first sight to be a series of compound arches – narrow, wide, narrow – but there is also a smaller, pointed arch almost hidden behind each rising roof rib. On this evidence there cannot originally have been a stone roof (Barker).

In the choir north aisle every window has been altered, some totally, but three of the original wall shafts supporting the roof above have survived. All the stones of the roof are beautifully cut and assembled.

The choir south aisle has suffered fewer changes. The Norman windows with their stepped sills date from Roger's time. Hidden, regrettably, behind the organ pipes on the south side is a fine carved head. Studying the stonework by the west door into the Chapter House suggests it to be an insertion into the original choir aisle wall. Does it date from the completion of the chapter house and undercroft? Some of the stones of the aisle roof ribs may be original, but the roof itself has been substantially rebuilt.

CHAPTER HOUSE (normally closed to the public)

This probably dates from Archbishop Roger's time, although the undercroft beneath is clearly older. At its eastern end are two massive buttresses. A former architect friend studied the complexity of this part of the church for years without being confident of any deductions he made.

The two fine pillars supporting the roof are early thirteenth century in style – did a similar structure once extend to the east end? Midway along the roof, the ribs have at one time been cut short. The Chapter House would then have been two bays wide all the way to the east end. The stone benches along each side of the room at the west end were used at chapter meetings and court hearings. It is noticeable that the most worn length is by a round window, where it would be pleasantly warmed by the sun. Until recent years, there was part of a third round window on the south wall just west of the transverse arch, but it has now been rendered invisible with a coat of plaster! The inner and outer circles are not concentric, so casting sunlight up on to the roof. The windows are not centrally located within the bays. Fountains Abbey has a number of round windows from around the same date.

The apse at the eastern end could be contemporary with the older undercroft beneath. The western end of this upper story is now the chapter house; the eastern end is a vestry. The wide arch crossing from north to south dates from the mid-twentieth century. At that time the pillars in the undercroft beneath were in a dangerous state and had to be replaced. The fine spiral wooden staircase at the eastern end was regrettably boxed-in around the same time.

One odd feature of the Chapter House is that the south wall is thicker at the east end than at the west end; so thick, in fact, that a two feet deep fireplace was created within it in Victorian times.

At one time a round-headed doorway led from the choir aisle into the eastern end of the room. Part of its head survives beside the later square-headed doorway and its profile is quite different from that of today's entrance at the west end.

It was probably the earlier of the two doorways and would pre-date the medieval dividing wall in the Chapter House, removed in the twentieth century. The door bears very fine medieval ironwork and to its right is a former wash basin for the priest to wash his hands.

Inside the recess and on the left, is a hole through which water was probably supplied. In the 1970s it still bore a fine lion's head (Fig 29), but that has been worn away by heavy vases of flowers being placed there. If the wash basin is the 'lavatory inside the choir door' mentioned in the minster accounts for 1408, it means that the round-headed eastern door to the Chapter House had already been altered by then.

Figure 29: lion's head in the Chapter House wash basin

At the south-east corner of the Chapter House and built within a buttress is a small chamber described by Hallett as a sacristy or treasury but which, in later times, has been a toilet communicating with a pit beneath (now panelled off) within the wall of the undercroft.

UNDERCROFT

From the outside (Fig. 30), it is obvious that the undercroft and Chapter House have quite different bay structures, in fact they have five and four bays respectively. Had the undercroft been designed after Roger's choir was completed, its ground plan would certainly have taken Roger's choir bays (and buttresses) into account.

Above the steps leading down to the undercroft is a good array of masons' marks, sadly becoming less discernible over the years with repeated painting of the ceiling.

The very feel of the undercroft sets it apart. Inside (Figure 31) there are small, crude windows and massive square piers to support the roof, so different from the elegant bases and capitals of the columns in the Chapter House (Figure 32). The two pillars were replaced in the mid-twentieth century. The corbels too, are totally different (Figure 33), as are the ground plans of the Chapter House and undercroft.

Lady loft
(later still)

Chapter House
(later)

undercroft
(early)

Figure 30: Chapter House and undercroft from outside

Figure 31: undercroft interior {now the Chapel of the Resurrection)

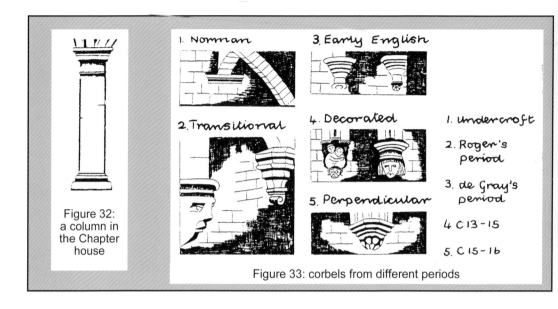

Figure 32: a column in the Chapter house

1. Norman
3. Early English
2. Transitional
4. Decorated
5. Perpendicular

1. Undercroft
2. Roger's period
3. de Gray's period
4. C 13 – 15
5. C 15 – 16

Figure 33: corbels from different periods

CHAPTER 12

The choir fall, Scots raids and then a prospering church (c.1260-1450)

BARELY THIRTY YEARS AFTER THE WEST FRONT was completed, the east end fell. It was hardly surprising: the terrain was sandy, the site sloped and building techniques that had sufficed for small Saxon churches were inadequate for the massive and soaring 12th-century walls. Despite their seeming strength, such walls were simply two thicknesses of dressed blocks with a miscellany of river cobbles, stone chips and mortar between. This is well illustrated by a portion of wall at the east end of the nave north aisle: when a Norman buttress was later removed, it revealed the rubble and cobble interior.

The choir's fall in 1280 affected the easternmost three bays on the north side and the last two on the south. Much of the east wall was itself rebuilt and although it has been suggested that the round scar over the east window pre-dates it, a likelier explanation is that it is where a stone rib formerly supported a timber barrel vault (Harrison). The part-arch at ground level outside was probably placed there to ensure that weight was supported by firmer ground.

An interesting feature of the choir's rebuilding (attributed to *Archbishop Romanus*) is the flying buttresses erected above the choir aisles, to counter the outward thrust of the choir roof. They would have then passed through the sloping roof outside the triforium and until a few years ago one buttress bore a scar from where the roof formerly abutted against it. The 'flying' or 'scientific' buttress was a significant advance in building technique (Figure 21).

The walls from the main arcade upwards had to be thickened and this in turn caused problems in joining the new work to the old; the three rebuilt piers on the north side are not in line with the axis of the nave! - a point missed by many observers. As already mentioned, three carved faces on the westernmost of these (northern) piers distract one's attention from the problems the masons faced (Photo 8, p.171). The capitals of the two arcades differ slightly from one another and the easternmost capital on the north side bears foliage in the 'Decorated' style.

Scott says that the rebuilding was completed by 1297 but in 1318, the minster suffered heavily in the Scots' raids with the stalls and screens being set alight (Parker) and thereafter, there were extensive repairs and additions to the church.

Hallett thought it likely that the spires and roof were renewed; Fowler states that restoration was still incomplete in 1328. Until late in the 19th century there was a date '1331' in the choir but on the evidence of two shields formerly there, Walbran dates the completion of work as post-1340. Gowland thought that the battlemented wall that formerly ran across the east end of the church (outside) was built after the Scots' raids. Perhaps the battlemented parapets were first erected then (Roger's roofs simply overshot the walls, above the corbel tables) for not only were the walls of the apertures angled to facilitate the firing of arrows, but the garderobes provided could have been used by the defenders (Harrison). Certainly, a man spent two days in 1354 'mending gutters round the church' and where there were gutters, there must have been parapets.

Outstanding survivals from the mid-fourteenth century are the glass medallions now in the window by the font (Photos 13 and 14, p.172; to be discussed in Chapter 20) and the single misericord seat depicting two men in fatal combat (Figure 34); although it may be of a later date. Perhaps the early set of misericords was surmounted by a canopy designed to ward off downward draughts. In later times canopies became decorative (like Bromflet's) rather than functional, as windows became more draught-proof.

The priests' seats *(sedilia),* (Photos 18, p.174) to the right of the high altar date from around the second quarter of the fourteenth century (Crossley). Animals and foliage are interwoven on the shafts and beneath the canopies are animals bearing human heads, each with two faces. In one recess, an anxious king is uncomfortably close to a sneering

Figure 34: the fourteenth century misericord

queen: could this be Isabella who deserted her husband (Edward II), then was involved in the invasion of England which led to Edward's unseating? - an early political cartoon. If Crossley's date is correct the carvings would have been highly topical, for Edward II was mainly to blame for the disastrous defeat of the English by the Scots at Bannockburn in 1314, an event contributing to the later Scots' raids on northern England.

The old roof bosses have survived several changes to the choir roof (Photo 23, p.177). The third from the east end shows Eve about to leave the Garden of Eden, followed by Adam who has the point of the angel's sword uncomfortably near the small of his back. In a lovely carving of the Annunciation, the figures of Mary and the angel are separated by a lily in a vase, representing the purity of Mary (see also Chapter 18).

It is not known whether the minster floor was of earth or stone at that time. There is a record of a man paving the floor for a day and a half in 1408, but in 1402, rushes were strewn on the Chapter House floor. Pease straw was used for the choir stalls later in the century, but they may have had a wooden floor.

Lady chapels were mentioned in Chapter 11. Scott believed the Ladyloft (above the Chapter House) to date from the mid-14th century and Fowler mentions 'the Lady chapel above the vestry' in 1391.

One of the earliest records in England for repairs to an organ comes from the minster's accounts for 1399. Two horse hides were bought for four pairs of bellows, as well as two skins of calves, three of sheep, some packthread and five hundred small nails.

Wood was bought in 1408 for the foundation of the 'purpytyl' but whether this was a rood loft or a choir screen, is not known. In later years there was an organ on it for which Richard Carver was paid 6d in 1453, to repair the 'groping mensal': probably, the keyboard.

Chantry altars were introduced from the early thirteenth century and Hallett records that, by about 1500, there were nine in the church. It was difficult to fit so many into a church that lacked nave aisles so there was not only one above the high altar and another below it, but seemingly, one in the roof above the north transept chapel!

The medieval alabaster carvings have already been mentioned in Chapter 5 (Photos 16, p.173 and back cover).

In the north transept, the tomb against the north wall is that of Sir Thomas Markenfield, soldier and Eleanor, his wife, and in the early nineteenth century when the inscription was still legible, the date was recorded as being 1483. The nearby tomb in the 'Markenfield Chapel' is actually older, despite its better condition. (Photos 19, p.175) The armour is finely carved and the collar of park palings possibly indicates Lancastrian adherence. At Hornsby church in Wensleydale there is a remarkably similar tomb, made for Thomas Markenfield's brother-in-law. It lacks the special collar, but clearly the two men had commissioned the same carver to make their tombs (Fig. 35).

By the south wall of the nave, near the font, is a raised stone which bears a carving in low relief of a man kneeling near trees and a lion nearby. Experts agree that it is fourteenth century and of a Flemish style but discount the romantic tradition of it being the tomb of an Irish prince who returned from Palestine with a lion. Greenhill has suggested that the John of Topcliffe recorded as a spicer in the 1379 Ripon poll tax record, could have had trade connections with the continent and may be related to the Thomas of Topcliffe, whose Flemish-style brass of 1391 is in Topcliffe church. Sadly, the carving has worn much, since Hallett pictured it in his book of 1901.

The west front was 'improved' in 1379 by placing mullions in the lancets but Gilbert Scott happily removed them.

Figure 35: detail from the Markenfield tomb
– a collar of park palings with a hind

Bells first appear in the minster's accounts in 1354 when Lawrence Wright mended the clappers, but considerably more information has survived from 1379. A bell, the 'Klank Knoll', was evidently bought from Fountains Abbey and it was taken, probably by sledge, to Boroughbridge, whence it was shipped to York for re-casting. The record includes buying poles for the bell frame, paying men working the windlass, buying 'messyng' (probably a mixed metal or bronze, used for mounting the bells), a pound of iron for the clapper, sea coal and finally paying the smith to make the clapper. All this work cost £11 10s 0d: well over £20,000 in modern money.

Having got the new bell to Ripon, 13lb of messyng was bought for two *coddes* (for mounting the bells) and … 300 'spykyngs grossis for the floor where the clock stands'. The old bell was removed and … 'two cordis pro les raypes' were bought, Will Fallan was paid 12d for a bell wheel and, in all, there was a further bill for £4 9s 0d.

There is an interesting entry for 1391. Sixteen stones of grit were bought for making a new metal casting hearth in the hall at Thorpe Prebend (probably on the site of the present house of the same name), 'to make a new bell', and the next year's account notes payment to Thomas Carpenter for making a wooden wheel. In 1393 John of Sutton, smith, was paid 20d for making … 'barr, stapeles and coddes' for the new bell, from his own iron. Finally, a few years later, William Wright was paid to hang two bells and mend others. Two more brass bolsters were bought (so clearly, the bells were much used) as well as 'pypes', presumably to carry the ropes through the ceiling.

Work by Thomas Carpenter in 1391 was mentioned, and by coincidence, a Ripon carpenter – Harvey – made a timber vault for Thornton Abbey in Lincolnshire in the same year. In Gilbert Scott's time, there was still wood carving in the north choir aisle bearing the date 1397, suggesting that Ripon may have already been noted for its craftsmanship in wood, leading us on to the next chapter.

CHAPTER 13

William Bromflet, master carver

AT FIRST SIGHT, THE DATE of the choir stalls is beyond doubt: '1489' is carved on the misericord seat next to the dean's and '1494' (in Arabic numerals) appears on the bench end at the bishop's stall. It is unusual for churches or their contents to be so easily datable, although in truth the work is not so much datable, as debatable! Dean Paul Burbridge pointed out to me some years ago that Ripon didn't have a bishop until 1836; that centuries were to elapse before Arabic numerals were in common use and finally, the bench end is not adzed, it is planed! It must be a gentle joke by Gilbert Scott during his Victorian restoration, like the queen in a rampart in the south transept with a sword in her left hand, and a grinning cat's head beneath. I suspect the bench end is mainly Victorian, but incorporating the fine human and animal carvings of Bromflet.

Who did the medieval work? The chance survival of a small book of accounts for the year 1520 (approx), called the *Paper Book*, is most fortunate. It records work done and wages paid over a period of several months to a number of men working with wood and including no less than three, surnamed Carver: William and Christopher (who each received the maximum daily wage of 6d) and Ranulph, who got only 4d. Two other men, Robert Dowyff and Radulph Turret working at the same time were each paid the lower rate of 4d.

At the very end of the *Paper Book* is a payment to 'William Carver alias Bromflet' (spelled elsewhere as Brownfleet or Bromfleet).

There is little doubt from the nature of the entries that William was the leading carver: his name usually appears first in each entry; he almost invariably had the more demanding tasks; he spent two days at York and four at Hull arranging supplies and finally in 1520-1, he probably received a bonus of 6s 8d for supervising other woodworkers (the Surtees entry is for William Corner, but interpretation of handwriting often leaves room for debate).

William Bromflet and his colleagues were working at the high altar and the book has entries like:-

- *Making and framing a shrine;*
- *Framing and carving a canopy for the Body of Christ;*
- *Framing panels and carving by hand the high altar;*
- *Trellising and carving;*

- *Carving and setting up works;*

- *Carving and cleaning images;*

- *Making a case for the sacrament;*

- *Trimming 'doriths', locks etc behind the high altar;*

- *Choosing, cleaning and bending timber;*

- *Making scaffolding and*

- *Sawing wainscot.*

The final entry is 'For 120 fathom long line for the conveyance of the shrine with two little lines called side ropes, 9s.8d'. Evidently they made a new reredos (backdrop) with carved images for the altar; a pyx to suspend over the altar with the Blessed Sacrament in it; and behind the altar, a new carved shrine to hold the head of St Wilfrid. Concerning the purchase of rope, a curious feature of the east window's frame today, is that high up on each side is a hole. Could the two holes have once housed ropes passing up to a device in the roof that would raise the cover of the shrine? It does seem likely. Perhaps too, the altar and reredos were not greatly unlike the high altar as we see it today.

The work recorded in the *Paper Book* was only a small part of the work done on the high altar, for the short fabric account for 1522 records substantial payments for the work and donations towards it. So much for the one project of William Bromflet, for which significant records have survived.

A few years before that, he had contracted to make a statue of St George on a grey horse, and a dragon. They were to be on a loft nine feet in width between the pillars 'adjoining St Wilfrid's closet'. The loft was to be ceiled beneath with oak and it was to contain an altar.

By comparing similarities of style and noting the re-use of certain motifs, Purvis has suggested that William Bromflet was responsible not only for the canopied stalls at Ripon, but for similar work at Jervaulx, Bridlington, Manchester, Beverley and (probably) Easby. Much of the carving was dispersed at the Reformation to parish churches under the patronage of the Scrope family: thus Aysgarth and Wensley to the west of Ripon have work attributed to Bromflet. Purvis noted that there was a remarkable degree of standardisation in the size of components (bench-ends, for example) from one of Bromflet's churches to another.

Apart from the Bromflet woodcarvers, John Bromflet was successively procurator, chantry priest and prebendary at the minster from 1531-1553 and Ranuld died here in 1557. Where did they all come from, York? If we refer to records of the Freemen of York we find that between 1337 and 1483, no fewer than 21 were Bromflets. Many were merchants whilst others had occupations like chapman, barber, maltster, weaver, clerk and chandler. Thomas in 1454 and William in 1463 were each Chamberlain of York.

Two sons of 'William, mercator' (i.e. merchant) were Freemen in 1478 and 1479, the nineteenth and twentieth of that name. The twenty-first and last (there were no more for at least a century) was 'William Bromflet, carver'– in 1483. A board in the Merchant Venturers' Hall at York names William Bromflet as Governor/Master of the Merchants and mercers of York in 1480/1

The Drawswerd family in York at that time contributed to an outstanding standard of craftsmanship, so is that where William Bromflet was trained? The dates do fit: if the York Freeman was also the Ripon carver, then it was just six years after becoming a Freeman that he and colleagues began creating Ripon's canopied stalls. Experts say that variations in style of the Ripon misericords suggest that they are the work of three carvers (we must exclude the two or perhaps three that are modern: the church today has 34 seats as compared with 32 in Bromflet's day).

Most of the misericords depict animals. What were the sources that inspired the carvers?

The earliest known scientific book on animals is Aristotle's, of the fourth century BC. Not long after that and probably in Alexandria, an unknown author compiled the *Physiologus* which with its emphasis on symbolism, was clearly not a textbook but a religious treatise. It achieved immense popularity and was translated into Icelandic and Persian, among other languages. By the end of the 13th century, bestiaries had widened in scope to include wonders of nature, and above all they were often superbly illustrated, offering themes to craftsmen working in wood, stone, tapestries and so on. By the 15th century (the time of our carvings) only one bestiary is known to have been written, reflecting the increasingly scientific attitude being taken towards the created world.

From an early date, animals had human characteristics ascribed to them. So the elephant was equated with chastity and on the bench end of the bishop's stall, the indestructible church (the howdah) is supported on the back of the chaste Mary (the elephant). A further moral touch is that 11 people are safely inside the castle while a twelfth – Judas – is firmly gripped in the elephant's trunk.

When the Jews were wandering northwards from Egypt, Moses sent out Joshua and Caleb as spies and 'they came to the valley of Eshcol and cut down a branch with a single cluster of grapes, carrying it back on a pole between them' – as the bishop's misericord shows. Unfortunately, they reported, 'the land was inhabited by giants' and they, too, feature on the misericord: one has no head, the other has a face on its body (Photo 20a, p.176).

The *Biblia Pauperum*, with its illustrations, provided 'copy' for the spies as well as for Samson carrying away the gates of Gaza and for the two fine carvings of Jonah: Jonah being cast to the whale and Jonah climbing back on to dry land. A collection of old prints dated 1826 includes one by either Martin Schongauer or a pupil of his, of a peasant pushing a woman in a wheelbarrow (Photo 20b, p. 176) and this, the Ripon carvers copied faithfully.

The underlying story must undoubtedly be that of Cuthman, said to have pushed his mother in a wheelbarrow until it broke at Steyning in Sussex and where he built a church. To this day, the church on that site celebrates annually the feast of St Cuthman.

On an adjacent seat the supporters (a dog and a woman) recall Simonides' cynical classification around 500 BC of women as mean and spying, and linked with bitches – from which we have one of the less pleasant epithets of the English language.

In pre-Christian days the lion represented an unsleeping guardian and so was often mounted in stone above gateways. The church adopted it as a symbol of good although curiously, in the service of compline, the devil is likened to a roaring lion prowling around 'seeking whom it may devour'. The lion is on the dean's stall.

Opposite it is the finest of all the carvings, on the stall of the canon-in-residence (Fig. 36). The oak bench end has a wonderful rippling grain and the carving of a scaly beast (or 'cockatrice'). Mr Whittaker, the Whitby woodcarver, once told me such wood is called 'tiger stripe', and is thought to be associated with trees that grow in very windy locations. I took many parties of wood carvers round the cathedral and mentioned this theory to them, without response. Then, only a few years ago, I met a party of woodcarvers from all over the world. I had barely begun telling them about the woodwork when a lady stepped forward and said "My country is Malaysia and I know where to find trees like this and which part of the tree to cut!" When Michaelangelo began work on a block of stone, he set out to liberate the spirit contained within his medium - which is precisely what the Ripon carver did in creating a scaly beast above the bench end, with its body reflecting the sinuous profile of the wood beneath.

Nearby, the divisions between the stalls clearly show the carvers' fitting marks and a point of interest in this area is the massive thickness of the bookshelf used by the boys in front. The carvers' humour breaks out at times, with a pig playing bagpipes and a fox (symbolising a friar) preaching to a gullible congregation of a duck and a hen. Nearby is a delightful variation on the usual foliated arm rests: one of them has instead, a grinning mouth. Pagan beliefs are mocked in the carving of the green man, a fertility symbol: he is depicted upside down and with animal ears.

The end stall on the north side bears an ape (Photo 22, p.176), which from early times was used to portray human follies. The seat today is the official seat of the Mayor of Ripon, who is solemnly installed in it each year, after commencing office. I know of no other English town that has such a ceremony.

The western canopies are original (fifteenth century) and those on the north side, outstanding: as is usual with medieval craftsmanship there is no mere repetition and they display fascinating variations of shape and detail from canopy to canopy.

Intricate tabernacle work mounted high up on the east end of each range of canopies, must have formerly been elsewhere in the church. Another notable piece of carving is the vine scroll mounted above one of the wooden screens by the choir north aisle: perhaps it relates to the 'trelissing' mentioned in the *Paper Book*?

Imported wood (from the Baltic, via Hull) supplied timber for panelling that had to be free from knots, but the wood for the misericords is almost certainly local oak, seasoned for five years or even longer. When a North Riding man called Thompson set up business as a woodcarver over a century ago, it is said that he was so inspired by the Ripon carvings that he adopted the mouse ('poor as a church mouse') as his trademark. Today, Thompson of Kilburn is known worldwide as 'the mouse man'.

Figure 36: stall of the Canon-in-Residence

CHAPTER 14

Ripon crafts and craftsmen

AS TO HOW THE CHURCH WAS BUILT, a few observations must suffice. By the twelfth century, the use of a 3-4-5 triangle was well established for setting out right angles on the ground and as building proceeded, the master mason could use a plaster tracing floor to explain the details required. Patterns were scratched on the floor with a pointed stick; they darkened with age and so the same surface could be re-used (such a floor was discovered at York Minster in modern times). From the early twelfth century, the foot was used for measurements and $16^1/_2$ feet made one 'rod', which is exactly the height of the first storey of Roger's nave. To control storey heights, storey rods were placed upright on the projecting string courses.

The *sandstone* used for Roger's church is said to have come from Hackfall up the Ure valley and would have been floated down the River Ure on rafts, some eight miles to Ripon: in modern times, the remains of ancient staithes have been found not far up the Ure from Ripon. For re-building the nave in the sixteenth century, 'quarries in Ripon' supplied the *magnesian limestone*: no less than £122 was spent on such stone in 1503 when the rebuilding commenced.

Before going any further, note the respective prices of three common raw materials:-

Lime $1^1/_2$d, lead $1^1/_2$d, and iron 9d per pound.

The source of the *lime*, used for lime mortar, is not known. In very recent times, an excavation just north east of the cathedral has revealed a substantial circular structure. Was it a lime kiln? – so far there is no agreement as to its original purpose.

Plaster was readily available from deposits on either side of the Ure, just north of Ripon; Roger's church was probably plastered throughout and it was only in Gilbert Scott's time that the badly decayed plaster was finally stripped away. In 1392, seven days were spent in bringing 18 cart loads of plaster to the minster (for making a new house, not for use within the church). The plaster cost 216d and transport was a further 105d, making a total cost of about 18d a cart load. The hire of a cart cost 15d daily, or roughly £125 in today's money, using the multiplier of 2,000 suggested in an earlier chapter. Four cart loads of firewood (cost, 51d) were bought for burning the crude calcium sulphate dihydrate into anhydrous calcium sulphate. Carts were a fairly recent introduction and some years later there is a record of two mules being used for transport.

In 1457 and 1458, the Fountains Abbey accounts record the purchase of bitumen from Ripon but there is no record of it actually being used here.

Local oak was used for most of William Bromflet's detailed carving but from an early date softwood – *'Eastland boards'* – were imported from the Baltic and an interesting record has survived from 1520. On 10th July, payments were made to William Howde for going by horse to Hull for four days and to William Carver, who was going to York on the 26th July for two days.

Payments were then made on the 31st July to Henry Wood of York for moving ...'100 waynscots and 200 clapboard' from Hull to York; to a Boroughbridge man for conveying them from York to Boroughbridge, and finally to five men who moved them in five carts from Boroughbridge to Ripon. When a second similar collection was made from Hull, cranage of respectively 12d and 4d had to be paid on the waynscot and clapboards.

Perhaps the best indicator to us of the carpenters' skill is the fact that the *'centering'* or framework needed for building a large window could comprise well over 100 pieces of wood. A close look today at the inner framework of the east window reveals that towards the top on the left, the curves are neither parallel nor smooth: it was no easy matter to select and shape the timber needed.

Principal doors would comprise two layers of boards, horizontal and vertical, secured by huge nails. Massive draw bars were used on the north, west and south doors as the rebates in the stonework still show (Fig. 37): the entire bar could be withdrawn into the wall. Thomas Turret had to make a new bar for the south door in 1393.

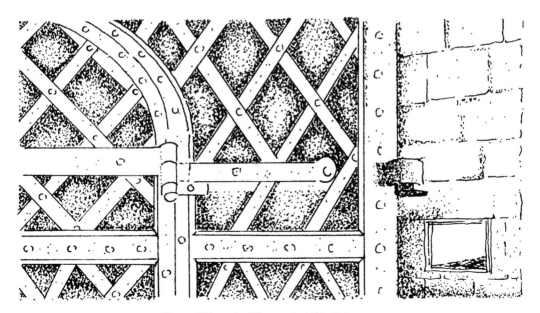

Figure 37: part of the central West door

Wood was bought in 1408 for the … 'fundo in le purpytyl' (i.e. pulpitum), which confirms the existence of an earlier pulpitum and for the door leading from it to the 'great organ'. The reference seems to be to the former small chamber in the pulpitum where the crypt exit now is, so was the pulpitum built, or only modified, after the tower's fall? Some anomalies in the pulpitum are hard to account for.

Thanks to Richard Wright repairing the door of William Loksmyth's chamber in 1478, we have a delightful example of the language used by the clerks of the day: Richard had to … 'sarracione vii gystez'! (i.e. saw seven joists).

Windows evidently had wooden frames at that time, for in 1391 and 1392, Thomas Carpenter mended faults in window boards in various parts of the church, including the great tower.

Lead cost only $^{1}/_{2}$d a pound, and had been worked in Nidderdale since Roman times: Wilfrid had used it to repair Edwin's church at York in the seventh century. Many of the surviving fabric accounts record work by the plumbers on roofs, gutters and windows and sometimes the plumber received a 'salary' (i.e. bonus) at the year end.

In March 1354, 300 lead nails (plumbers' nails with leaded heads) were bought and John was paid to cast lead and work on the roof. With lead from the church store, Richard Bettes made … 'guturas cum spowtis' for the new chamber over the Chapter House in 1392: so the Ladyloft was then still incomplete. In the following year, one sixth of all Fabric Account expenditure was on the purchase of lead: 1,680 lb, costing 60s. Unfortunately the accounts for the next two years have not survived so we don't know how the lead was used.

A few years later (1399) William Bettes supplied 560lb of lead and there were purchases of tallow for plumbing and glazing and 8lb of tin, for mending 'glass windows' and making plumbing solder for various window panes.

The Fabric Account for 1354 illustrates just how much work was sometimes needed for maintaining the church's windows. In March, William Glazier began mending windows damaged by … 'grossos ventos'. He continued throughout the month and two bushels of lime were bought … 'for the fixed glass windows (N.B. "fixed") and for pointing'. April, May and part of June passed in the same way, then the account relates that Lawrence Wright and six other carpenters spent six days taking down the scaffolding in the choir. We cannot assume that William had been working there, for medieval accounts are just that: disjointed narratives, never intended to present a logical picture of what actually happened.

Although *iron* was very costly, there seem to have been no problems in getting supplies, and iron working at Fountains is recorded as early as 1195. Iron was in constant use for making door catches, locks, keys and hinges: from 1354 there is a record of new locks and keys being bought for the 'vicedores' (i.e. the doors to the winding stairs) and for the chamber in the pulpitum.

John Mimersmith made two chains in 1392 for fixing two 'Ordinals' to the choir stalls, they were the books of rules governing the choice of service, day by day. He also supplied a thurible and chain for burning incense at funeral services.

In the following year, Robert Marshall supplied:

> *14lb of iron for the church store, at 9d a pound.*

Thomas Wright used it to make:

> *1,000 spykyng grossis, 1,500 lead nails, 5,000 stane-brodds* (pegs for slating house roofs) *and 100 big nails.*

New *bokettes* were needed periodically for the well, and were usually banded with iron. In a fine piece of archaeological work just south of the minster a few years ago, the pits were revealed in which vats for dyeing or tanning had been sunk: the pit wall clearly showed where iron bands had circled the vats.

Charcoal was used for iron making throughout the Middle Ages but in 1453, the smith doing work at the minster used sea-coal: that would have been for the blacksmith's fire. Iron working had so developed by 1408 that three iron chairs were bought for use in the choir. They must have caused a sensation and with leather cushions, were perhaps not uncomfortable.

There can seldom have been sufficient work at the church to warrant employing a silversmith or goldsmith full-time, but 'Widone aurifabro' is named in a late twelfth century document and at a later date, there is mention of work in silver at the high altar. At the Reformation, silver from the shrine was sold at York for £21.

In 1354, 18 stone or more of *cannabis* was bought at Selby. Cannabis was hemp, and Robert Raper of Ripon used it to make cables for work in the church and a rope for the well in the cemetery. A rope was purchased initially, to tie the cannabis to the horse's back. When further cannabis was bought in subsequent years, it was made into ropes for the bells, shrine, well, tent and *veil* (the veil across the high altar at Lent: the hooks for suspending it from the choir pillars are still there).

CHAPTER 15

The tower is shaken and the nave falls (c.1450-1540)

IT WAS SHOWN IN CHAPTER TWELVE that only a few decades after the late Norman church had been completed, it suffered first the collapse of the east end then devastation by the Scots. Some thirty years later, Black Death miserably afflicted the townspeople. Many years elapsed before all the vacant properties were again inhabited, then in 1450 disaster again struck the church.

The inherent weakness of the centre tower's design and some early difficulties with its north-east corner, have already been noted. In 1450, it was the south-east corner which suffered an earth tremor. We don't know the extent of the damage (Fig. 38) but the canons decided to rebuild the adjacent stonework in the choir and south transept in the perpendicular Gothic style, using magnesian limestone. Skilled masons must have then been hard to find, for some of the work is very crude, when compared with the craftsmanship of Roger's time. Until 2010 there were lights on top of the pulpitum shining upwards and one was very aware of the marked irregularities of tooling.

Worship in the minster was obviously out of the question and there are references in 1450 and 1459 to services being held 'in a little chapel hard by': possibly the Ladykirk, to the north-east of the minster. How were congregations accommodated, for the greater festivals?

The rebuilding of the two walls of the centre tower entailed the refashioning of three piers and two of them today project out into space with superfluous flat upper surfaces, intended to carry the last two pointed arches (Photo 4, p.170 and Photo 11, p.171). A fascinating feature of the north-east pier is that on its top, one can see exactly how stones would be assembled to support the new pointed arch on the north side of the tower. Like the south transept, the standard of masonry is not high.

The fragmentary records available, coupled with the fact that so often the accounts describe what sort of work was done, but not where it was done, make it impossible to give a firm chronology for this period.

So in 1459, Richard Bramhowe left 6s 8d to the fabric of the great tower 'which is to be made' while in 1453, £29 (a substantial sum) was spent on carpenters, sawyers and plumbers repairing the roof but as to where the work was done, one can only guess. Perhaps the centre tower, because indulgences were granted for work there in both 1465 and 1482.

Drawing by one-time Canon Residentiary James Ashworth

Figure 38: an impression of the damage caused by the fifteenth century earth tremor

From 1502, a slightly clearer picture emerges. The nave, which had been threatened with ruin in 1482 was now *'very much in ruins'* and rebuilding of the south side began shortly afterwards with Christopher Scune – who also worked at Durham and Louth – as the master mason. £122 was spent on stone in 1503 and £80, two years later, all of it coming from the magnesian limestone quarries at Ripon. The sale of indulgences made a modest contribution to these costs.

The nave was described as ruinous in 1512. Catastrophic bulletins did help to prick the consciences and open the purse strings of the faithful! That same year, 50s was received from the canons, singers and vicars for the foundation of *'le north Ile'* (of the nave) and money was given for a mass celebrating the laying of the foundation, on the 2nd September.

In 1505 an appreciable sum was spent on *'carr. le bones'* and bones were still being carted away in 1523 and 1525, probably from where the south aisle of the nave was to be built. Many went into a big pit at the east end of the churchyard; the choicer ones were put in the undercroft beneath the Chapter House.

It seems likely that, without either vaulting over the aisles or completing the centre tower, attention switched to the south side of the choir, where the west end was rebuilt in an elegant Perpendicular style.

The triforium arches with their perpendicular tracery were given round heads to blend with earlier work in the choir. Near the tower, Roger's work was probably simply encased in limestone; the original sandstone survives on the aisle side of the wall, bearing masons' marks common to Roger's period. Half-way down the choir however, a main pillar was totally removed and higher up, there is a striking 'straight joint' where the new work was not bonded into the old.

It is interesting to compare how the masons opened up the transepts to the new nave aisles. On the earlier south side, the connecting arch has the same height as the main arcade to the nave and cuts intrusively into the transept's triforium; the masons had obviously used one of the timber formers made for the nave. This fault was rectified when they came to the north aisle and built an arch of height appropriate to the storeys of the transept.

Throughout the Middle Ages there was a relentless drive towards new and 'better' fashions and the new nave clearly shows this. Although little more than 10 years separate the two nave aisles, there are many differences between them: the height of the first string course (and hence of the windows); the profile of window frames and the patterning of mullions; details of the main pillars and the profile of the main arches. The two humorous faces of Figure 39 may date from this period. Fowler's verdict on the new nave was 'exceedingly good', replacing 'the very curious structure of Archbishop Roger'!

The shafts between the aisle windows bear figures above, some with shields. One is of Archbishop Bainbridge of York who became a cardinal in 1511 (hence, the cardinal's hat) and another is of his predecessor, Archbishop Savage, 1507-1511.

It was not until the 19th century that the lean-to roofs of the aisles were replaced with stone vaults. Buttresses like those to the new nave south aisle (Figure 40) could never have been imagined in Roger's day.

Besides all the work by the masons, Bromflet and his associates spent some time around 1520 making a new high altar and a figure of St George on horseback (Chapter 13).

It seems inconceivable that after the fall of part of the tower and the rebuilding of it, of part of the south transept, part of the choir and most of the nave, more trouble could arise: *but it did.*

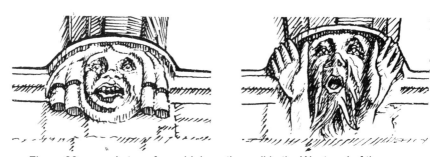

Figure 39: carved stone faces high up the wall in the West end of the nave

By 1537, the Chapter House was described as 'ruinous in walls, roof and stonework generally' and in the following year the Archbishop of York met Christopher Dragley (Treasurer), Marmaduke Bradley and others to consider the matter: Abbot Bradley (see Chapter 4, 'The end?') now held two keys to the Chapter House and he promised £4 yearly from his prebend towards the cost of repairs. The fine iron work on the east door to the Chapter House probably dates from before Bradley's time.

The only Fabric Roll to survive subsequent to 1537 is that for 1541 and no mention is made of work on the Chapter House, so presumably it was complete. One obvious source of trouble

Figure 40: buttresses on the nave South aisle

would have been the Chapter House vaulting and although the ribs are probably original (they bear masons' marks common to other fabric from Roger's time), the stones of the 'web' between the ribs have certainly been placed in an unusual pattern near the west door of the Chapter House. No stone vaulting was being done in the church at that period and the skills may not have been available. Perhaps it was then, too, that the undercroft vaulting was strengthened by adding extra ribs.

Now, let's consider the *pulpitum*, (the stone screen that separates the Choir from the Crossing). It's known that there was a pulpitum prior to 1408. I have seen sandstone blocks beneath the current pulpitum (which is, of course, limestone) and, some time after the tower's fall, the pulpitum was re-modelled. The statue niches are of varying width and the two outermost ones are markedly narrower, to give added strength to the structure. It has been suggested that perhaps the pulpitum came from another church but I think things are sufficiently complicated without that hypothesis; anyway, nobody has suggested the previous location! A notable feature of the screen is the representation of Christ in majesty in the triangular space above the centre doorway, surrounded by delicately carved figures. Below two of the main figures, the shields of Ward and Pigot are easily recognisable, and on another shield is a merchant's mark with initial W: this might be either Wakeman Wilby (1476) or Wakeman Whare (1472).

In the 1970s, when I used to take school parties around, the children often sent me individual thank-you letters enlivened with drawings. One lad said he liked especially … 'the angel on top of the screen, playing an electric guitar'!

If the re-fashioning of the tower led to problems for the masons, did William Bromflet and the woodcarvers meet similar difficulties because of changes being made to the eastern piers of the tower and to the choir?

It's noteworthy that the geometry of the carved canopies differs in layout from the southwest to the north-west corners: notice the relative positions of the two posts in the corners, supporting the canopies. One misericord is dated 1489 and the bishop's bench end is '1494': but both dates must be jokes of Gilbert Scott's in the nineteenth century, for centuries would elapse before local people used Arabic numerals! Moreover, the church was not a *cathedral* (with a bishop) in 1494. It seems a fair assumption that having begun work on new choir stalls and canopies in 1489, it would all be kept in store pending completion and subsequent assembly. Below the return stalls, on the north side are the carvers' fitting marks (until modern times one could see similar marks on projecting roof timbers of a building in Shrewsbury but the timbers were all sawn off on Health and Safety grounds!).

Bromflet was a highly skilled craftsman and moving his work into place should have been no problem yet it was so: look at the junction of stalls and return stalls on the south side. Compared with the join on the north side, the work manifests clever improvisation to get it all in. Bromflet was perhaps overtaken in his work by what the masons were doing on the tower.

From posterity's point of view, it is fortunate that the Reformation did not arrive either earlier, or later. If later, the urge to have a church resplendent in the latest fashion would have produced one of the finest naves and crossings in England, but where would the process have stopped? The church is undeniably an architectural mongrel, but one of great character. Had the Reformation come sooner, essential stonework would have been incomplete and the church could conceivably have been abandoned: certainly, there was no money available in succeeding decades for any reconstruction on the scale of the early 16th century, for most of the church's wealth had passed to the State.

Before leaving that part of the church, it may be mentioned that in 1466, the church had a fine processional cross, carrying the figures of Our Lady and St John. Hallett remarks that the Dean's Verger's mace 'has been ascribed to the fifteenth century' and wondered whether it had once been borne before the town's wakeman. In 1468, the book *Pupilla oculi* was to be chained to the stall of the prebendary of Monkton, on the north side of the choir: perhaps this was the same book as the Ordinal, mentioned in 1392.

In the crossing stands an old stone pulpit to which no date has been ascribed (Photo 36, p.185). Moody says that changes to the church in 1872, showed that the pulpit had once stood on the northern side of the pulpitum but to judge by its style, it could be older than the pulpitum.

This raises the question: 'what is the age of the pulpitum?' Fowler thought that the 'purpytyl' of 1408 (mentioned in the last chapter) was the pulpitum, and that does seem likely, but Scott believed it to be much later. Parker makes the interesting comment that 'Practical masons are of opinion that the screen has been placed in its present position subsequently to the erection of its flanking pillars, though it is the older structure'.

Could Fowler, Scott and Parker all be right? One very obvious anomaly to the screen is the carved detail below the two outermost figures, which is both cruder than the rest of the carving and is of different material. It is also notable that the three innermost figures on each side are of similar width, whereas the outermost niches are narrower, but different from one another (Photo 26, p.180 and Appendix 6). The decorative frieze along the top, too, has an improvised look to it, as the two ends do not match. Again, a small detail, but the shaft descending to the floor to the right of Athelstan almost looks as though it had not been made originally for that position. Finally, in the archway behind the choir doors, there is a distinct hint of two periods of masonry.

CHAPTER 16

Exit the spires
(c.1540-1676)

EDWARD VI's REIGN WAS MARKED AT RIPON by the arraignment of staff for their loyalty to Catholic ways (Chapter 5), but in Elizabeth's reign which followed, the church was badly damaged by soldiers, following the Rising of the North.

In January 1572, John Norton and two others visited the church to assess the damage and report to Sir Ralph Sadler, Chancellor of the Duchy of Lancaster. They met plumbers, carpenters, a smith and a glazier and found that the lead roof was ... 'in great decay' because, in the late rebellion ... 'the queen's soldiers took lead off the gutters of the "middle ile", so that water now runs down the walls'. Downpipes had been hacked off and the lead of the three spires was much decayed. They estimated that four 'fothers' of lead (a little over four tons) would do no more than repair the damaged areas. Other estimated costs were £3 6s 8d for ropes and other engines; £6 13s 4d for timber needed to replace rotten wood on the spires, to put beneath the lead and to replace doors and windows burned by the soldiers; £5 for glass, lead and solder for the windows; £6 to replace locks, keys and iron bands stolen by the soldiers and £26 13s 4d, in all, for labour: Such was the price paid for the rebels' freedom to say mass in the old way during the rebellion.

More destruction followed in 1575, when Sir William Mallorie and Rafe Tunstall were ordered to pull down the 'gilden tabernacle': almost certainly the fine work of 1520 onwards by William Bromflet.

Heaven-sent (as opposed to man-made) trouble struck the church in 1593. At 3am on 5th May, ... 'the great spire of St Wilfrid's steeple was set on fire by lightning. By God's aid and the help of men from the town it was quenched before 7 am'. Working in the dark and without hosepipes, it would have been hazardous.

The records become fragmentary at this point but late in the sixteenth century, Robert Dawson was held responsible for the decay of the nave and in 1600, Sir William Mallorie and others were commissioned to enquire into the state of it.

Moses Fowler became Dean shortly afterwards but his memorial (... 'not a favourable example of seventeenth century Gothic sculpture') was soon to be mutilated in the Civil War, as were those of Sir Thomas Markenfield and Anthony Higgin (in the library): Higgin is renowned for having established a fine collection of books at Ripon (although the chaplain William Rhodes had left money to the church in 1466 for books that were to be stored in a screened-off part of the Ladyloft).

A reminder of the period is the copy of the *'Directory for publique worship'*, which was formerly in the Cathedral library.

Altar rails became popular in the seventeenth century, both to curb the irreverence often shown in church in Elizabeth's reign (the earliest graffiti in the Cathedral is from that time) and to exclude dogs. A careful look at the nave rails shows that two lengths are much older than the rest and formerly had balusters about 4in apart (to exclude the dogs). It has been suggested that they may originally have been in York Minster.

The centre spire survived until 1660 then crashed in a storm, wrecking much of Bromflet's work on the south side of the choir. Walbran says that the spire was octagonal, 120 feet high and with four spurs, each 21 feet high. Medieval carpenters showed great skill in creating spires with timber frameworks that could take the stresses arising in gale-force winds (Figure 41).

Charles II authorised an appeal following this disaster and his letter related that the chancel – 'the only part where the people could assemble for worship' – was smashed down and the body of the church was 'sorely shaken and much weakened'. The estimated cost of repair was £6,000 but seven years later (1668) only £1,262 had been raised: that included £100 from Archbishop Sterne, grandfather of the novelist Laurence Sterne.

Parishes in Durham, Yorkshire, Cumberland and Lancashire gave only £9 in all: Easington in Co. Durham sent a 'Parliament 6d', a bad penny and several *bodwells* (a bodwell was a copper coin worth a sixth of a penny). Parliament money was nearly worthless, '£10' of it realised only 16s. Mr Pinkney was given £1 for his expenses in going to see Lady Anne Clifford, who responded by writing to the mayor of Ripon and Sir Edmund Jennings, offering £20 towards the appeal.

As the money flowed in, so work began and, in October 1661, wood worth £80 was bought from Sir Richard Mallorie, followed by much more in succeeding years. Lead purchased from 1662-6 cost £226.3s 8d. Workmen's pay, formerly from 4d to 6d a day had risen to about 3s to 7s a week. Lime, on the other hand, had fallen to a third of its former price, by virtue of the minster having its own lime kiln, perhaps located at either Quarry Moor or Whitcliffe, on the edge of the town. Or possibly, just to the north east of the Cathedral? In April 1666, 16s 9d was spent on … 'coals and wood pro lime kiln'.

Figure 41: impression of the west front before the fall

Hair was bought on various occasions, $2^1/_2$ bushels of it in 1664, and there are two references to purchase of water bags, also needed for making mortar.

Early in 1662, William Carnaby replaced glass in the choir and Chapter House, and thereafter much work was done on the windows, probably including replacement of windows smashed by the Roundheads several years earlier. The noted York glazier, Henry Gyles, was busy on the west window in 1664, ... 'painting in glass the inscription of King James' foundation' and ... 'painting in glass the king's arms'. It was reported that ... 'sixty odd bars of iron' were bought for windows in 1665.

Several years later, James Coats was paid 7s 4d for a chain for the 'king's arms', which Mr Whithill painted: perhaps this was the James I coat of arms that now hangs in the south transept. It was cleaned in modern times by Clerk of Works Jack Yarker, using "Lux" soap flakes.

Considerable work was done on the bells. The first payment was of £20 in May 1664, to 'Mr Smith, Bellfounder in part'. In August, agreement was reached with Smith on casting a new bell and Matthew Townley put all the bells into new frames in November. Finally in December, £28 0s 8d was paid to Smith for 841lb bell metal at 8d a pound.

Work began on a new organ in December 1663, with an initial payment to Mr Preston of £5. His final bill for £30 in April of the following year brought his charges to £100 in all and then 7s 3d was paid in June for painting the pilasters on the organ top. Some of the old pipes, which are inscribed in German, support the tradition that Gerhard Schmidt – who had a child baptised in the church – was associated with the seventeenth-century organ. Parker says that 'an organ' was built by Schmidt in 1695-6, but would Preston's organ have had so short a life? It is more likely that Schmidt added extra stops to Preston's organ.

The present console is too large to fit into the original organ balcony (which is probably late seventeenth century). With his back to the singers, the organist could use a foot pedal to move the wooden hand up and down, and strike the beat for them. I once explained its use to a visiting organist whose choir was to rehearse for Evensong. When he operated it at choir practice (it can be moved by a lever in the present organ loft) the choir fell about with mirth: it was not used for the service!

For three years work went on intermittently in paving the floor of the church. In March 1666, Gill and Rainford were paid ... 'at a new bargain' of 22d a yard for getting, bringing, squaring and laying stone. Two years later, Gill was paid for 166 yards, which included work near 'St Wilfrid's closet', and near the south door of the choir.

The accountants' problems with arithmetic in the Middle Ages have been noted earlier. The account for 1663 has an apologetic footnote:

> 'Mem^d y^t y^e is a mistake here in the accounting, & it should bee 57-12-08 because 38-07-02 taken out of 97-19-10, ye remainder is 59-12-08 and not 57-12-08 as is here set down'.

Locks and other fastenings were bought for the lead house and the charnel house: what was the function of the latter? On a lighter note, crows were clearly a problem around the church because a few years later, Edward Harrison needed powder and shot for killing them and William Lumley's gun needed mending. In my time at the Cathedral the clerk of works was busy up in the centre tower one day and saw a pigeon on a lower ledge so raised his gun and shot it. The bird's body fell down to ground just as a lady emerged from the choir!

It was unthinkable that further trouble should arise if one of the western spires were to fall, so the dean went to London to see the Secretary of State and obtain the King's permission to remove them. He paid a fee of £6, plus 6s … 'pro solliciting the busynesse'. A bizarre episode occurred during their removal. Matthew Townley, in charge of the work, was being held by workmen near the top of the spire, on ropes. Matthew's eye fell on two men racing their horses on Bondgate Green and perceiving that the hindmost rider was holding back his horse, cried out 'Let go, let go'. It was Matthew's men who let go. Matthew fell …'from the top of the spire to the top of the tower', and was fortunate to be merely badly bruised.

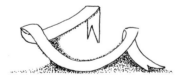

CHAPTER 17

The choir is transformed
(1660-1828)

THE SPIRE'S FALL IN 1660 severely damaged the choir, including Bromflet's stalls and they were re-fashioned sometime afterwards; but precisely when this happened is not known. A minster account book for 1661-1676 has survived, and makes no mention of the stalls but like all surviving accounts, the location of work done is seldom specified. Many of the canopies had been destroyed and the choir interior was drastically changed by inserting box pews and galleries. In the Middle Ages the choir accommodated only singers and clerics, but the new fittings (later removed by Scott) could seat almost as many people as the entire church does today. Obesity was not much of a problem in those days!

In 1862, Walbran noted that, since 1646, there had been a support for the mayor's mace beside the first choir stall on the north side. In Walbran's day, most of the north side stalls were occupied by the 'Municipal Corporation', the mayor's seat being behind the monkey. Perhaps the singers had seats in front; this subject will be returned to in Chapter 18.

In December 1663, ale was bought for workmen removing the choir ceiling. Next month, there was an initial payment to Lawrence Brown relating to the ceiling and a further £3 soon afterwards. In June 1664, 3s was paid for … 'glue and paper for the roof of the choir'. Finally a year later, glue, turmeric and saffron were used … 'for painting in the choir'. Regrettably, we cannot tell whether this was only a small operation, or a larger one, for which many details have not been recorded.

Candlesticks were bought for the pulpit in 1665, followed by varnish, size, blacking, wax and glue for the pulpit cover. Then a cushion was purchased, as well as … 'looplace for the cloth'. Several years later, Mr Whithill was occupied in painting and colouring behind the communion table; the altar rails were mentioned in the last chapter. The 'silver verge' bought for £2 13s 4d in 1662 was perhaps the one carried today by the Canons' Verger.

The £1,262 raised towards the restoration included over £6 contributed by 12 people in respect of pew rents, which were becoming an important source of income and appear in one of Heneage Dering's account books, early in the following century. In parish churches at this time, it was customary for the churchwardens to allot seats to parishioners, according to their status.

Workmen were paid 10s in 1668 … 'pro designe of battlements & turretts', but whether they were for originals or replacements is not known (battlements were considered in Chapter 12).

A fine set of communion plate was given to the church in 1674-6 and the 'cups, patens, flagon and *aire'* (a 3-footed cover to place over the paten and bread) are held today in the cathedral treasury. Parker speculated that it may have first been used at a re-opening service, following the church's restoration.

As part of her tour of England on horseback in 1697, Celia Fiennes came to Ripon and remarked upon the town's cheap meat and dear inns. She also described a red and gold painting over the altar. The church possesses a fine red and gold frontal, thought to date from not long after the time of her visit; it has four panels of flowers but when seen at a distance of a few paces, two of the panels take on the appearance of fiendish faces. Could this have been made to match the 'picture'? The town council by now met regularly in one of the choir galleries and councillors paid 2s 6d each to sit there.

At the end of the eighteenth century, an engraving by Wood (dated 1790) depicted the battlemented east wall formerly located just east of the east end and containing both a door and a window. Perhaps intended as a fortification against the Scots, it was partly demolished in 1790 and completely removed in 1830. By then, a further gallery had been added … 'to complete the north side gallery' (Smith).

When Thomas Dibdin met Dean Waddilove a few years later in the library and rummaged among the dusty books and cobwebs at a temperature of 81^0F, he was astounded to discover two Caxtons: Boethius' *Consolation of Philosophy,* plus a delightful English-French phrase book for merchants and travellers. In recent times, there was a further surprise when Mrs Mortimer of Leeds University found Caxton's *Epitome of the Pearl of Eloquence*. Two of the Caxtons were sold in order to establish the Cathedral Choir School in 1960.*

Early in the nineteenth century, Ripon gained from York the statue of James I that now stands beneath the north-west corner of the centre tower (he was replaced at York by Henry VI). Until 1850, James stood over the entrance to the south choir aisle.

Late in the 18th century, the sculptor Nollekens made a marble bust of William Weddell the owner of Newby Hall (for display in the Hall). The design is based upon a fourth century Athenian monument. A few years later, he created a copy for the minster's south transept. An entrance porch in the classical style was erected outside the Norman south doorway, probably around the same time. Depicted in one of Wood's engravings, it was removed sometime in the following century, perhaps when the extra order of roll moulding (noted by Barker) was added to the Norman doorway.

In the early 18th century, not all the floors were stone-flagged but floors were re-laid in 1804, mostly with new flags. The walls inside were repaired and repainted at the same time.

A Consistory Court for use by the chancellor of the diocese had been set up in 1722 at the west end of the nave north aisle. Early in the 20th century, it was used by the bishop.

> *** Editor's note***: *the choir school closed in 2012*

As part of his restoration, on the court's west wall Gilbert Scott placed the dark stained wooden canopy, probably made in 1808 by a local man for the bishop's throne in the Choir.

In Wood's engraving of 1790, the west towers have neither battlements nor pinnacles and these were first added around 1797 (the pinnacles were removed in the mid-twentieth century). The drawings also show the Y-tracery in the west lancets, which was removed by Scott. A new clock was installed in the south west tower in 1809; it had the first face to be visible from the street.

The famous angler's epitaph was noted earlier in the book. Other memorials, now lost, included ones to Margaret Lupton (d.1718, was mother and grandmother to over 150 children), to Henry Raper (d.1728):

'Here Henry Raper/Lies in dust/His stature small/His mind was just'

and John James Cook of Newby (d.1760):

'Who was a faithful servant to his master and an Upright downright honest man'.

Memorials in the next century were to be much more fulsome, but perhaps less realistic!

CHAPTER 18

Blore's alterations

and

Scott's restoration

(c.1828-1900)

ALTHOUGH SOME NINETEENTH CENTURY RESTORATIONS were undeniably unfortunate, the restorers of the time were hardly the vandals that some of their contemporaries and some later writers have suggested. What was the nature of their inheritance?

Hudson has described how at Ely Cathedral (in 1750), the nave was used by coal carts as a short cut and when somewhat later Charlotte Brontë visited Filey church, she found that the walls were green with mould and most of the paint had flaked off the pews. When parson Atkinson first entered the church of his new, moorland parish in north Yorkshire, he was appalled to find that the communion table had a broken leg and it was covered with a ragged cloth on which were stale breadcrumbs. It was not only the fabric of churches that was neglected at that time.

George Gilbert Scott's restoration at Ripon (1866-1871) followed only some 30 years after Blore's (c.1830-1834), yet he found that the north-west tower was then an empty shell open to the weather and the roofs of nave and transepts were in so poor a state that rain poured in, 'as old folk remembered' – to quote a later writer. The pulpitum was green with mould, while the nave north aisle was used by a local builder to store timber: and in winter, to mix mortar.

From these examples, one begins to appreciate the difficulties faced by restorers. Total restoration pre-supposes the availability of money and skills and whilst Scott had, for example, woodcarvers who could restore Bromflet's 15th century work, Blore probably had not.

The neglect that Blore found in 1830 must have far exceeded the fund-raising capacity of the day, neglect characterised by a minster which for many years had had no confirmation service and where one dean fled the country leaving the church's finances in disorder, whilst another was noted – among other things – for the time he devoted to literary research in Spain (Chapter 6).

Most of Blore's changes were swept aside by Scott, so how sensitive was Scott to the past? Of the west front, Scott himself wrote ... 'The three western portals had gabled terminations, which have been nearly obliterated. These have been restored, the old forms being accurately discovered and preserved'. Again, referring to the choir galleries, Scott wrote ... 'beneath them were a series of enclosed pews, which had been formed in part of some interesting old work, of which I could not ascertain its origin. This I earnestly begged should be preserved, but I fear it has been since dispersed'. Let us allow the last word on the subject to Dr Edwin Crow, cathedral organist in 1877, who complained that Scott ... 'unfortunately refused to move the screen (i.e. the pulpitum) which now cuts the cathedral in halves'. Crow was exasperated at having to sit at a console high up on the pulpitum and added ... 'a more absurd position could hardly have been devised' but he was also echoing a fashionable outlook of the day: 'away with screens'.

Within 50 years in the nineteenth century, the church's choir had no less than three roofs. Of the first – the seventeenth century roof – Tuting said that it was flat, was several feet below the top of the arch (a strange feature, yet in a drawing of the south transept by R. Douglas, around 1800, the lower part of the upper Gothic window projects below the ceiling) and it had a blue sky sprinkled with both small clouds and gold stars. At each corner was a large cherub with wings; there was a sun at the east end and a moon at the west. Blore replaced it with a lath and plaster roof and Fig. 42 must date from after his restoration. Note that it shows the bosses at the rib intersections: Parker says that, in the seventeenth century restorations, the bosses from the broken roof were put into store in the Chapter House and later used by Scott in his roof. Probably Blore had done likewise, thirty years earlier.

A notable feature of Blore's work was the lengthening of the east window (Photo 33, p.184) to its original proportions; it had probably been changed when the battlemented east wall was erected. For the enlarged window, the *Yorkshire Gazette* noted in 1830 that ... 'the additional coats of arms which have been given for the purpose have been admirably executed by Mr Willement of London': who also made the Norton window in the nave north aisle and signed it 'TW' in the lower right-hand corner. Willement's coats of arms are among those now in the library east window (which for some reason was totally re-arranged sometime after 1860).

Gowland relates the interesting history of the (high) altar, which for three-and-a-half centuries was the church's only altar. In the 17th century it was moved back to the east wall – having formerly stood one bay westwards – with Bromflet's reredos behind it. As the latter was so badly damaged, it had been concealed by a painting of an Ionic colonnade by Streater, the sergeant painter to Charles II. Walbran says that having designed a new reredos to replace the painting, Blore removed the latter and found Bromflet's reredos (although Tuting claimed the credit for that) which he thereupon discarded.

Figure 42: how the Choir probably looked before Scott's restoration (etching by Buchler)

That, in turn, revealed that the arcading at the sides of the choir continued under the east window (Gowland) as Fig. 42 shows and it was removed by Scott: a bewildering sequence of changes. I believe that the Streator painting was in the cathedral until the mid-twentieth century when it, too, was discarded.

One of Blore's changes must have created a stir in Ripon when in 1830 the oil lamps used to light the building were discarded in favour of gas. It was not until a quarter of a century later that heating stoves were put in the church and an under-sexton was paid £1 a year for looking after them.

In the transepts, Blore applied papier-mâché vaulting which Scott described as pre-dating the Norman walls below.

Critics did not take kindly to Blore's new internal deal roof in the nave. Parker merely described it as an 'inappropriate flat roof of 1834' but the *Yorkshire Gazette* of that year spoke of the 'ugly flat ceiling'. Most likely, there simply was not the money for a more sympathetic treatment of the nave roof: the initial appeal had raised £5,000 but the final bill exceeded £6,000.

The bishop's chair which used to stand in the high altar sanctuary is an interesting piece of work by a Ripon craftsman in 1850; where is it today?. Old wood was used except for the mitre and finials, and the side panels matched the carving at the back of the south misericords, facing the Chapter House door. Notice how, in Fig. 42 (Buchler), there is a decorative band along the front of the stalls on the north side. Could this be similar old work, which Scott managed to preserve?

I believe past writers have underestimated the part played by Dr William Goode. As dean from 1860-1868, he clearly worked with great commitment preparing the way for Scott's restoration; work that ultimately cost five times as much as Blore's. Perhaps too, the skills of the dean and Sir Gilbert Scott in launching the appeal have not been fully appreciated. At a meeting called in Ripon Town Hall on 4th October 1861, Scott presented a report that envisaged spending £17,000 on a new nave roof, improvements to the ceilings of transepts and choir and - a task never actually undertaken - spires on the west towers. Provision was also made for lighting and heating. A subscription was started and £10,000 promised there and then, equivalent to an immediate 59% attainment of target, although as time passed, the scope – and cost – of the work increased markedly.

At the east end of the church, Scott's main achievement was to restore the external roof to its original pitch and to insert beneath it the oak roof that we see today, complete with its (mainly) medieval bosses (Photos 23, p.177). These are described in Appendix 7.

Another substantial task was the removal of all galleries and the restoration of Bromflet's canopies and misericords. How much of the woodwork today is medieval and how much Victorian? If one looks at the canopies in bright light, it is evident that the easternmost eight on each side – 19th century work – have wood that is smoother and darker in colour than the rest. Then looking at the upper canopies on the north side it appears that a few pieces of the older, lighter wood have been used by Scott's craftsmen as patterns for the restoration.

At least two misericord seats are modern but many more have been extensively and very skilfully restored, often ones that were delicately carved.

If one stands today at the west end of the stalls, near the dean's stall (giving the aspect depicted in Fig. 42), it is at first difficult to reconcile the bench ends with those in the engraving because at least five shown there have gone: the three crocketed ones at left and centre foreground and the two at right front, each with two (and not four) lancets. Of the 24 present today, 16 have plain faces but 8 are carved, in every case on a basic pattern of 4 upper and 4 lower lancets. The eight carved bench ends are:-

> 1,2 Bishop's stall (with elephant) and the bench end in front.
>
> 3,4 Dean's stall (with lion) and the bench end in front.
>
> 5,6 Canon-in-Residence (scaly animal), and the bench end in front.
>
> 7,8 Mayor's stall (monkey), and the bench end in front.

From the studies of J. S. Purvis it is highly probable that bench ends 1, 3, 5 and 7 – at least – are original, but would that more early detailed drawings existed! Whatever the ages of the bench ends, one has to admire the skill of Scott's craftsmen in recapturing the feel of Bromflet's choir (Photo 25, p.179), when so much of the original work was missing.

Fig. 42 clearly shows the galleries in the north choir aisle. The south aisle was similarly galleried and was used by the Sunday School. It was entered from the steps leading to the library: the access door still exists, hidden behind the organ pipes. The windows above that aisle had earlier been blocked up and Scott re-opened them; he also repaired the roofs to both choir aisles.

In Blore's time (see Figure 42) there were three steps up to the altar, but the rest of the choir floor was level. Scott introduced a step up, just east of the misericords (in pre-*Health & Safety* days), and the new raised portion shows fine fossils (crinoids) in the blocks of the inlaid pavement. The westernmost area was re-laid, with the pattern running diagonally. The piscina and sedilia on the south side were moved from the penultimate to the last bay and new, high pinnacles were added. At that time too, the brass lectern with its eagle was purchased. In the course of all this work, a medieval stone altar with five consecration crosses was found, but, unbelievably, was subsequently lost!

The steps to the library were badly worn and Scott prepared to renew them but discovered that the adjacent wall to the left bore a fine medieval painting (Photo 40, p.186), so replaced the staircase a short way from the wall (Photo 30, p.181). In the library itself he put a new pine ceiling but re-used the oak corner pieces from a previous roof.

In the transepts, Blore's papier-maché ceilings were removed and the 15th century ceilings 'restored or reproduced'. Beams inside the north transept (above Scott's flat ceiling) are massive and medieval but the corresponding structure in the south transept is of iron. One feature of the ceilings that has escaped the attention of previous writers is the painted, carved wooden figures that support them. Some in the north transept relate to 19th century benefactors as their shields testify, but other figures in the transepts include a man with the Pigot coat of arms, one with the Norton arms, St Peter (crossed keys), a man with a pipe, one with two pitchers, one with crossed swords, man with lute, a man with a basket of five round loaves and an extraordinary carving of a queen in a turret with a

sword in her left hand and with a cat's face beneath the turret (Figure 43 and Photo 39, p.186), clearly echoing the story of Alice in Wonderland.

To add to the mystery, an undated newspaper photograph (c.1870?) shows four of the figures, then unpainted, resting on the floor against the pulpitum: St Peter, Norton, the pipe man and the man with two pitchers. Were these four, at least, figures that Scott had found abandoned or hidden somewhere in the roofs? And did he then set his carvers to make more figures in a similar style? It seems likely.

Figure 43: Queen with sword

Walbran had commented in 1862 on Blore's papier-mache transept ceilings and said that *'their contemptible character was aggravated by grafting new capitals on the old shafts, in a style wholly inconsistent with the original design'.* In other words, the carved figures that we see today beneath the transept roofs were not there before Scott's restoration.

Finally, was the Queen with the sword a whimsical touch of Scott's? 'Lewis Carroll' – Charles Lutwidge Dodgson – had visited Ripon regularly when his father was canon at the cathedral and it was while Scott was working here that Dodgson negotiated with the Revd Badcock, principal of Ripon College, for the artist Tenniell to use Badcock's young daughter Mary as the model for 'Alice' in his stories. It must have caused a sensation in town, of which Scott would have been fully aware and if he had a sense of humour at all akin to Dodgson's, perhaps he resolved to have a carving that would baffle posterity: despite widespread appeals, nobody has come forward with a rational explanation for it. The queen, the castle (chess), the sword in the wrong hand ('Through the looking glass') and the cat's face (or severed head: 'off with her head'), all have an 'Alice' flavour.

Until that time, there were still timber roofs on the nave aisles and Scott had them replaced by stone vaults, drawing on stone which had been stored in the church (presumably since the 16th century). The flat deal ceiling in the nave was replaced by the present fine oak ceiling with its many bosses (Photo 41, p.187). It was made to the same design as the transept ceilings at York Minster: but whose head is it, depicted on a boss near the east end? It is remarkable that the work was done without disturbing the exterior roof, even though in places the two roofs touch one another (*Ripon Gazette*, probably in or about July 1872).

In Scott's restoration, considerable craft skill was allied to modern civil engineering: the process for example of inserting a huge iron girder 60 feet or so up in the north wall of the centre tower must have been watched with admiration by the townspeople.

 Much greater problems had to be overcome at the west end, where successive interments beneath the towers had so undermined the foundations that they had to be supported temporarily with huge baulks of timber, before underpinning the walls to a depth of 12 feet. There were severe fissures in the towers' fabric and the men worked in peril of their lives, with at one point a great mass of rubble breaking away from the wall above them. 'Thank God it was effected in safety', Scott wrote later.

As to the final stages of the operation, I can but repeat the story told me by an old Riponian, which he in turn heard from someone present at the time. In order to remove the final baulk of timber, it was soaked in tar then set alight. The bolder or more curious onlookers had all assembled at a safe distance on the far side of Bedern Bank, expecting that the towers would crash down – but were disappointed.

The towers' floors were restored and additional strong iron tie bars inserted: presumably the existing ones dated from Blore's restoration.

A few years ago, in the masons' shop, I saw one of the huge, original spanners used for tightening the bars. At the highest level and just below the west gable, the bars coming to the centre from each tower are locked into a massive forging. Strong blocks of stone replaced the fissured fabric and they were held in place by copper bars.

A comparatively minor job at that end of the church was to remove from the west windows the decayed mullions, which had been secured by wooden beams to stop them falling out. The work aroused considerable controversy at the time, although the mullions were well over a century later in style than the lancets that framed them.

One piece of new technology around 1895 seems to have had a short life. The present official guide to Fountains Abbey is that written by R. Gilyard-Beer who was an eminent twentieth century Ripon historian and whose father had a greengrocery shop on the west side of Bedern Bank. He, with typical Victorian enterprise, bought an electrical generator which was delivered to his premises by horse and cart from Ripon railway station and from which a single electric cable was taken across the road to provide lights in the cathedral. Probably the system was too unreliable to gain permanent acceptance.

Constance Cross was born in Ripon in 1851 and was, with her sisters, a noted benefactor in the city. Late in that century, they gave to Ripon the clock tower which stands at the junction of Palace Road and North Road (and which was for a time under threat in the interest of traffic management) but in 1895, she presented to the cathedral the white 'Agnus Dei' altar frontal which is now rarely used but can still be seen in the altar frontal cupboard. A few years later she gave another frontal made by herself and other Ripon ladies but there is no record as to which one that was: an old green frontal was restored around 1990 and there is also an old purple frontal in occasional use. The wooden screen that stands alongside the north choir aisle was made by some Ripon ladies of whom Constance Cross – noted as a carver as well as embroiderer – may have been one. The screen incorporates some delightful fragments of Bromflet's work.

A few years after Scott's restoration – in 1878 – a new organ by Lewis replaced Gerhard Schmidt's. It worked by water power, and the door at the top of the library steps gave access to the bellows. It was not, like modern organs, susceptible to power failures, but its noisy mechanism was a drawback. In building this new organ above the pulpitum, the old stone pulpit then standing there was taken down and placed at the entrance to the north choir aisle.

The recent record of fonts is confusing but in Hallett's book (1901) there is a picture taken at the west end of the nave south aisle. The octagonal 'marble' font stood then (as now) on two steps, and behind it on the floor was the old circular basin, that in the 1970s stood in the south-west tower. Tuting had discovered it in 1842, in a garden just north of the cathedral. It was subsequently dumped outside, for the second time, a few years ago! That font is of particular interest, because it dates from the time when baptism of infants was by immersion.

Happily, the twice-dumped font now serves as an altar in the Chapel of St Peter, choir north aisle (Photo 27, p180). According to Walbran, the 'octagonal font of blue marble' had stood until 1722 just inside the west door, before being moved to its present position.

A third font appeared in the Millenary Book's record for 1871. It said that a new font of fossil marble was put in the north-west (*sic*) tower, … 'the gift of the Canons who were anxious to restore the old one'. It is not mentioned by either Hallett or Parker, and one has to assume that like the classical doorway formerly outside the south transept, it had a short life.

By the end of the century, the Dean and Chapter were studying specifications and quotations for lightning conductors. Having once stood just inside the south-east corner of the church as lightning rattled down inside the fabric, I marvel that the church – even without spires to further attract lightning – should have escaped serious damage for so long.

Figure 44: the West front today

CHAPTER 19

The twentieth and early twenty-first centuries

UNTIL THE TWENTIETH CENTURY, the church's sole altar was against the east wall, but a bequest in 1906 enabled the Dean and Chapter to establish the St Wilfrid Chapel in the choir north aisle (now renamed St Peter's Chapel).

The nave had been in regular use for worship since the latter part of the 19th century and in 1913, the present bronze pulpit – by Henry Wilson – was installed (Photo 34, p.185). It is not clear whether the four figures of Cuthbert, Chad, Hilda and Etheldreda were planned from the beginning or were an afterthought, because the inscription –

'The gift of Wal / ter How / ard Stables Vicar / of St / Chad /

Far Headingly 1896 / 1906 / Ad / Maiorem Dei / Glor / iam'

has an improvised look to it.

The three fossils above St Hilda's head constitute an amusing blend of Christian tradition and 19th century tourism (Photo 35, p.185). When Hilda, one hot day, could no longer abide the many snakes that frequented her cliff-top abbey she banished them over the cliff edge where – allegedly – they were decapitated on hitting the rocks below. Twelve centuries later, Whitby boomed as a holiday resort and enterprising local traders collected ammonite fossils on the beach and carved snakes' heads on them, for selling to holidaymakers. (I believe that the original sounding board over the pulpit was a former table top from the Deanery, the present board dating from Sir Albert Richardson's restoration in the 1950s.)

There also occurred around this time the removal of the upper floor at the west end of the choir south aisle, which formerly held part of the organ mechanism. The oak choir stalls that were placed just west of the centre tower, survived until their replacement in the late 1980's by the present stalls.

The next significant addition to the church was in 1922-3 and 'created a lot of controversy', as an elderly parishioner told me some years ago: it was the high altar reredos in memory of those killed in World War 1 (Photo 37, p.185). The central figure is a youthful, clean-shaven Christ with a banner representing his victory over sin. He is flanked by St Michael crushing the serpent (i.e. evil) and St George killing the dragon: both horribly realistic if seen from the window sill behind.

Beneath Christ are the Virgin and child and to either side of her, figures from the Saxon, Celtic and Roman churches, respectively (Appendix 4). The separate statues of St Peter and St Wilfrid date from the same time.

Why was it controversial? Apart from the obvious reason of 'don't like change', two other objections would be likely. Firstly, this was a step away from the Protestant – almost Puritanical – approach to church furnishings which was still so prevalent in the Church of England and, secondly, it would be seen by many as clashing with the unpainted and ungilded choir stalls (the angels' heads on the organ balcony were only gilded a few years ago). Yet in the Middle Ages, it was normal to paint and gild wood carvings and in a sense the reredos – totally medieval in style – is more 'correct' than the canopied stalls. Ninian Comper was the architect, 'Mr Gough' the sculptor and Barnard Smith the colour artist.

Twenty years later more colour (and Catholicism) was added in the shape of the statues of Our Lady and the Archbishops Roger and de Grey, above the entrance to the south choir aisle. (Photo 28, p.180).

The last innovation of this kind was the placing in 1947 of figures in the stone screen. . (Photos 26, p.180, Photo 29, p.181 and Appendix 6). Knowing the desperate financial plight of the church from about 1546 onwards and its inability to complete even basic work like the roofs to the nave aisles, it is most improbable that statues were ever placed in the pulpitum and the new figures – even if some have very solemn faces – do, with their colour and gilding greatly enliven the church. The figures are the work of Esmond Burton. One Sunday afternoon in the 1980's an elderly gentleman approached me as I stood near the screen and said, with a smile, that he had done the gilding in 1958 (not 1959 as the guide books say). Mr Geoffrey had chosen a coach tour from London that stopped in Ripon so as to see his handiwork, which was done at a time when gold leaf was 12s (60p) a book. What better objective for a coach tour?

By this time, the fabric was again giving cause for concern and Archdeacon Graham raised £150,000 in 1955, for a restoration that was directed by Sir Albert Richardson. The work included building a masons' shop, work on the transept ceilings, replacement of much external stonework (for example, in the central tower) and strengthening the south side of the undercroft and Chapter House. The old transverse wall that divided the Chapter House was removed and replaced by the round arch which conceals a stainless steel saddle, inserted to stabilise the outer wall.

The next major internal change was the conversion of the choir south aisle in 1970 into the Chapel of the Holy Spirit. Leslie Durbin created the metal work which captures the feeling of Pentecostal fire, when the disciples received the Holy Spirit on the first Whit Sunday. (Photo 51, p.190). The sacrament is reserved in the pyx (Fig. 45) suspended over the altar, as was customary in France and England in the Middle Ages. The chapel is especially impressive after dark as one walks up the nave south nave aisle towards it.

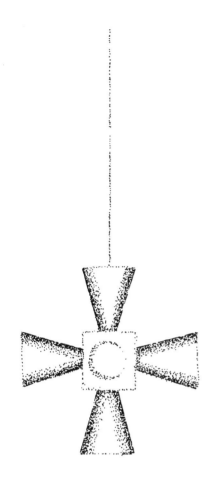

Fig. 45: the pyx hanging above the altar in the Chapel of the Holy Spirit

Chapter 1 mentioned that the body of Willibrord of Ripon now rests in the basilica of St Willibrord at Echternach, Luxembourg. In the choir north aisle, by the entrance to St Peter's chapel, is a wood carving bearing St Willibrord's name. It perhaps came from a war-damaged church on the Continent, some time after World War 2.

An outstanding aid for music in the cathedral was the gift by a former lay clerk of a portable organ console for the Harrison and Harrison 4-manual organ. It replaced an electronic organ which for a few years stood at the east end of the nave. The new organ was first used for the Christmas services in 2000 and can be placed west of the pulpitum with the audience seated behind the organist, so creating a totally new musical experience. The possibilities were dramatically demonstrated in 2007 by a young German lady who enhanced the occasion with athletic displays of arms and footwork. Frequently these days, recitals are given with the organ on the usual site of the nave altar. For one such recital, the organist, deputy organist and organ scholar all took part and in one piece, all three participating!

Happily, in 1984 the old pre-Conquest drum stone mentioned in Chapter 10 was moved into the eastern apse of the undercroft and the newly-named Chapel of the Resurrection was suitably furnished for regular use (Photo 43, p.187).

Just as Blore's restoration of 1830 was followed 30 years later by Scott's, so Richardson's of 1956 was followed at a similar interval by the work directed by Neil Macfaddyen and made possible by the appeal initiated by Dean Christopher Campling. With over £1m raised by 1993, it concentrated on the replacement of exterior stonework. Sandstone slowly suffers wind-erosion – a good example is the interior of the Norman chapel in Durham Castle – but limestone at Ripon has deteriorated sharply in recent years, with substantial amounts becoming rotten and fragile. In the nave, it reached the point where large wooden panels had to be fixed in the clerestory walks to protect people below from falling chunks of decayed mullions and the entire tracery of some windows was renewed. Considerable work was needed too on the parapets and the whole of the west front was cleaned.

Worn magnesian limestone (in mullions, for example) was replaced by similar, hard stone from Cadeby near Conisborough, whilst for gritstone replacement, the source was Bramley Fall, at Bramhope near Leeds. The mortar used comprised two parts of riddled grit sand plus one part of slaked lime, with a very small amount of white cement.

The blocks were squared on machine saws near the quarry but all subsequent work was done by hand in the cathedral masons' shop. The only concession to new technology was that pneumatic hammers were used for much of the cutting (instead of the traditional mallet); otherwise techniques were almost unchanged from medieval times. The local community takes pride in the fact that the skills of Ripon craftsmen have given the church a sound start to the next century (Photo 17, p.173).

Mention was made in Chapter 10 of the powers exercised by the new *Care of Cathedrals Measure*. Every Anglican cathedral is now subject to the oversight of a local fabric committee, to which any proposed changes of a permanent nature must be referred. That committee must, in turn, refer any major proposals to the Cathedrals Fabric Commission.

The high standard to which the cathedral is maintained today would astonish some bygone Deans.

Outstanding recent work has included total replacement of all electric wiring in the church to provide low-energy lighting, which can be varied automatically according to requirements; and – the gift of a local benefactor – provision of a superb exterior floodlighting system (Photos 53, p.191). Unlike older systems that (expensively) swamped the stonework with light, the new, energy-efficient system has the subtlety to reveal features long unnoticed. The effect is seen at night from whichever direction one approaches Ripon! At the same time, the public address system was replaced.

The year 2008 saw the fitting of three additional bells to the bell-chamber in the south west tower (Photo 50, p.190), taking the previous diatonic ring of ten bells to a 'light ring of eight'.

Safety is paramount in all aspects of running and using the Cathedral.

CHAPTER 20

Windows

THE GLASS IN THE WINDOW BY THE TUDOR FONT (Photo 13, p.172) was probably made by *Master Robert le verreour* who made the west window at York Minster in 1338 and the shield in the font window is that of the Earl of Cornwall, 1329-1334, with its three lions and blue 'label' (Diana Balmforth). Glass technology was by then well advanced: Robert the glazier knew for example the precise ratio of nickel and cobalt needed in the melt to give grey glass and he was fully acquainted with the newly-discovered art of silver stain, whereby glass – whether plain or coloured – was painted with a silver salt and re-heated, thereby causing its surface to change chemically to yellow silver silicate. The technique opened up endless design possibilities, because yellow patterns could be superimposed upon a base colour.

Medieval windows were primarily a teaching medium and St Peter with his keys is instantly recognisable. St Paul bears a sword (the instrument of his death) and St Andrew is shown with arms and legs outstretched, the posture in which he was crucified. The dachshund in the lowest right medallion can only have been created as light relief!

These fragments of medieval glass that had survived the 'Great Rebellion' (Walbran: 1643?) were made in 1724 into twelve medallions that were mounted high in the east window. In the mid-nineteenth century they were moved to the nave, in World War II to the Saxon crypt for safety and finally in modern times they were restored by Peter Gibson of York.

From the 15th century there are two delightful lozenge-shaped panes in the library that were probably among the glass bought by Sir W. Cummerland (a priest?) from Fountains Abbey at the dissolution (Fig. 46).

The next glazier of note to be associated with Ripon was Henry Gyles (1645-1709) of York and in one library window, are fragments of his James I coat of arms and the blue and gold 'Honi soit' garter which he made for the west window.

Figure 46: a medieval stained glass lozenge

The inscription 'Samson Staveley AD 1664' in one of the north transept windows is probably Gyles' work, likewise the jumbled fragments dated 1664, near the pulpit.

William Peckitt (1731-1795) of York provided new glass in 1791 in the great east window then when Blore lengthened it to its original proportions around 1830, Willement provided additional coats of arms for the new lights. Some 20 years later the whole window was reglazed by Wailes (1853). Just a few years before that, Charles Winston had published a book on glass painting that heralded a dramatic advance in the science of stained glass, which had much declined in quality since the Middle Ages. Many of the panels removed in 1853 were put in the east window of the library.(Photo 38, p.186) If one numbers the three ranks of panels as 1-5, 6-10 and 11-15, then panels 3, 8, 10 and 14 are not by Peckitt (T. Brighton) and may be by Willement: his work was also mentioned in Chapter 18. The window in the library with the arms of Norton Lord Grantley (whose chaplain was Waddilove, dean from 1792-1828) is by Peckitt (as are probably the pieces of red and yellow glass at the centre of the rose, in the great east window). Panels 6 and 14 in the library were restored by Septimus Waugh in 1978 and some years later the whole window was plated for security.

Towards the end of the nineteenth century, the lower half of the great east window was reglazed yet again with colours clearly superior to Wailes' apostles above. Red was a particularly difficult colour in the nineteenth century and for the central figure of Christ the robe is not a straight red glass, but either 'flash' or 'streaky' (two techniques employed for reducing the density of colour).

The relationships between mason and glazier must be touched upon here. Norman windows gave the glass artist no problem, for he had an unrestricted rectangular 'canvas' with a round head. But the reticulate glazing bars of the Gothic style could be torture to the glazier: few canvas artists in their right minds would attempt a picture that was several times as high as it was wide (there is for example, a very uncomfortable vertical group portrait in the nave south aisle, near the font).

Different windows excel at different times of the day and year, but the west window is so often inspiring, especially when the sun is behind it. There is an Impressionist touch in the top right corner, where the flames of fire are in varying colours. When sunshine pours through the green background to the window, it washes the left-hand nave pillars and the pulpitum in tranquil green light then as the day progresses, other colours in the glass become dominant. Late on summer evenings, one is conscious only of vivid red splashes on a golden yellow background. How well, too, the glass artist related his subject to the adjoining architecture.

In the nave south aisle, the window containing the Nunc Dimittis and the Nativity was put in less than 20 years after Wailes' twelve apostles (which Hallett described as ... 'very poor glass') and clearly shows the Victorians' rapidly growing mastery of glass colouration. Some paint is nearly always applied to windows in order to give, for example, details of faces and patterned fabrics and the two early 20th century windows in the

'Markenfield Chapel' were obviously made by an artist with considerable skill in that field: the glass received several applications of paint, with stoving between each application.

In the choir, the two easternmost windows on the side of St Peter's chapel (choir north aisle) date from 1870. Unlike any others in the Cathedral, they have the property of still retaining some light, even on the dullest days. Another striking feature about them is the way that the leading has been inserted so as not to conflict with the design. I believe that William Morris of the Pre-Raphaelite movement was associated with the glassworks where they were made and there is a strong Pre-Raphaelite touch to one of the windows in the nave north aisle, where the womens' faces have the same stark simplicity as that favoured by for example Millais and Rossetti, earlier in the century.

Warren Wilson's 'Ruth and Naomi' window of 1957, upstairs in the south transept, is very different in style and gives some pleasing colour effects, as sunlight moves across it. (Photo 46, p.189).

By contrast, Harry Harvey's 'St Wilfrid' of 1977, in the 'Markenfield Chapel' (Photo 48, p.189), uses some uncoloured glass and very little paint in order to minimise the exclusion of light – a lesson that the Victorian glaziers were slow to learn. It also greatly reduces the cost!

At the west end of the nave north aisle is a fine modern window by John Lawson of Goddard & Gibbs, in memory of Jean Emmerson whose husband supported the Cathedral in many ways (Photo 45, p.188). It cleverly challenges traditional (artistic) concepts of Christ's racial origins.

Part 3

OTHER INFORMATION

APPENDIX 1

Deans, past and present

1. Deans of Ripon (King James I Foundation)

Moses Fowler	1604 –1607/8 *
Anthony Higgin	1608 –1624
John Wilson	1624 – 1634/5
Thomas Dod	1635 – 1645
John Wilkins	1660 –1668
John Neile	1673 –1675
Thomas Tullie	1675 – 1675/6
Thomas Cartwright	1675/6 – 1686
Christopher Wyvill	1686 –1710/1
Heneage Dering	1710/1 – 1750
Francis Wanley	1750 – 1791
Robert Waddilove	1792 – 1828
James Webber	1828 – see next table

* Until 1752, the first day of the Civil or Legal Year was reckoned to be 25th March, known as Lady Day (significantly, nine months before Christmas Day). Dual dates shown above have the Civil Year in which a dean was appointed, moved on or died, according to the style of the time, followed by the historical year as reckoned today. Thus, 1675/6 implies a date between 1st January and 24th March 1676, but considered at the time still to have been in the Civil Year 1675; so, although Thomas Tullie was appointed in May 1675, he is recorded as having died in January 1675 – which was 8 months *later.*

APPENDIX 1 (continued)

Deans, past and present

2. Deans of the Cathedral

James Webber	(see previous table): 1847
Hon. Henry Erskine	1847 –1859
Thomas Garnier	1859 –1860
William Goode	1860 –1868
Hugh McNeile	1868 –1875
Sydney Turner	1876
William R. Fremantle	1876 –1895
Hon. William H. Fremantle	1895 –1915
C. Mansfield Owen	1915 –1940
Godwin Birchenough	1941 –1951
F. Llewelyn Hughes	1951 –1967
F. Edwin le Grice	1968 –1984
Christopher Campling	1984 –1995
John Methuen	1995 – 2005
Keith Jukes	2007 – 2013
John Dobson	2014 –

APPENDIX 2

Bishops, past and present

1. <u>Bishops of Ripon</u>

Eadhed	681 – 686
Charles Longley	1836 – 1856
Robert Bickersteth	1857 – 1884
William Boyd Carpenter	1884 – 1911
Thomas Drury	1912 – 1920
Thomas Strong	1920 – 1925
E. Arthur Burroughs	1926 – 1934
Geoffrey Lunt	1935 – 1946
George Chase	1946 – 1959
John Moorman	1959 – 1975
S. Hetley Price	1976 – 1977
David Young	1977 – 1999

2. <u>Diocesan Bishop of Ripon and Leeds</u>

John Packer	2000 – 2014

3. <u>Area Bishops of Ripon</u>

James Bell	2015 – 17
Helen-Ann Hartley	2018 –

APPENDIX 3

Naming parts of the Cathedral

It is impossible to write about a historic building without running into problems of nomenclature. In the text of this book, the current (2018) names have been used for chapels and similar discrete areas. However, names can be changed over the years and some areas may be known by both older and more recent terms.

Listed on the next page are the present names, followed by some of the earlier ones. Refer to the numbers in the plan below:

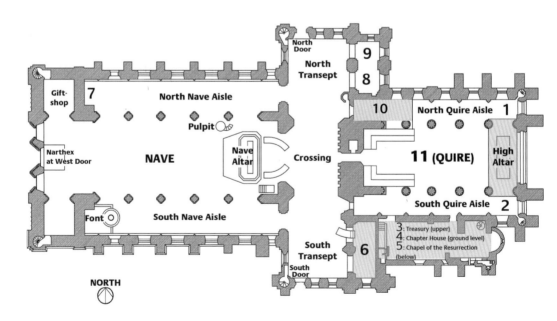

APPENDIX 3 (continued)

Naming parts of the Cathedral

1. St Peter's Chapel *was* St Wilfrid's Chapel

2. Chapel of the Holy Spirit

3. Treasury and Library *was* Lady Chapel (*or* Ladyloft)

4. Chapter House *and* Vestry (*not open to the public)*
    apsidal east end was once Lady Chapel

5. Chapel of the Resurrection *was* Lumber store *was*
    Bone House *or* Ossuary

6.   Service room (*not open to public*) *was* Mallorie
    Chapel *was possibly* Lady Chapel

7. Chapel of Justice and Peace *was* Consistory Court

8. St Wilfrid's Chapel *was* Pilgrim Chapel *was part of*
    Markenfield Chapel

9. Mothers Union Chapel *was* part of Markenfield
    Chapel

10. Service area (*not open to public*) *was* Treasury *was*
    part of North Choir Aisle

11. Quire *and* Quire Aisles *were* Choir *and* Choir Aisles

APPENDIX 4

Figures on the reredos

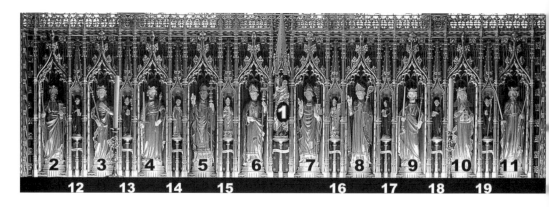

(see also Photo 37, p. 185)

No.	Subject	No.	Subject
1	Virgin and Child	12	The Venerable Bede*
2	King Alchfrith	13	Benedict Biscop*
3	Queen Ethelburga*	14	James the Deacon
4	King Edwin*	15	St. John of Beverley
5	St. Paulinus*	16	St. Cuthbert**
6	St. Augustine*	17	Eddius*
7	St. Columba	18	Caedmon
8	St. Aidan*	19	Alcuin
9	St. Oswald*		
10	St. Hilda*		* see Chapter 1
11	King Oswy		** see Chapters 1 and 2

Continued ...

APPENDIX 4 (continued)

Notes on selected reredos figures

Alchfrith, son of **Oswy**, provided the land at Ripon for founding a monastery

Edwin was the first Saxon Christian king of Northumbria

Columba, from Ireland, founded the monastery at Iona

Oswald: after being killed in battle, King Oswald's head was ultimately put in Cuthbert's coffin

Oswy, baptised at Iona, succeeded his brother Oswald as King of Bernicia and, by marrying Edwin's daughter in 643, united the royal families of Bernicia and Deira (northern and southern Northumbria). He presided at the Synod of Whitby in 664

James the Deacon stayed at his post in 633, when Edwin fled south

John of Beverley ordained Bede as deacon and priest

Caedmon, an unlearned monk at Whitby, saw a heavenly vision that led him to write Anglo-Saxon scriptural verse

Alcuin, born in 735 and educated in the cloisters in York, became a particularly eminent scholar on the continent.

APPENDIX 5

Carvings under the misericord seats

There were only 32 seats in the Middle Ages, as against 34 today (see Chapters 4 and 13). Proceeding clockwise from the bishop's stall, the 34 are:-

Position of choir stall	Image below misericord (for more detailed interpretations, see *Medieval Woodcarvings of Ripon Cathedral* in the Further Reading section of this book)
1	(The Bishop's seat): Ripon (with Manchester) became a cathedral again in 1836, England's first cathedrals since the Reformation. Caleb and Joshua are watched by two grotesque figures, either *Blemyae* (as in Hereford's Mappa Mundi), or *Anakim* (from the Old Testament account of the Jews' wanderings). (Photo 20a, p.176)
2	A head – probably from Scott's restoration work. The earlier Bishop's stall was double in width but had only one misericord. On its division into two stalls, this new misericord was needed.
3	Samson carries away the gates of Gaza.
4	Jonah emerges from the whale's mouth. The two-legged 'mouse' to his right is a typical medieval touch.
5	A pelican feeding her young, flanked by two ugly heads with protruding tongues.
6	A hart, chained.
7	A griffin, a mythical winged animal, half eagle, half lion.
8	A fox stealing a goose; a woman with a distaff on one side and a dog on the other.
9	St Cuthman wheeling his mother in a barrow (Photo 20b, p.176).
10	Jonah is thrown to the whale. The carver must have been familiar with the conquest of perspective, first achieved by Brunelleschi and Masaccio, half a century or so earlier.
11	Piglets dance as another pig plays bagpipes.
12	A mermaid with mirror and brush warns the spectator of earthly vanities.

Position of choir stall	Image below misericord
13	An owl. In the darkest corner of the church, it denotes the Jews, either because they walked in darkness through not having seen the light of Christ, or, at an earlier date than these carvings, they only left their homes after dark for fear of persecution.
14	A griffin devours a human leg.
15	A lion and a griffin fighting.
16	An angel with a shield dated '1489' – and clearly not done by the same carver as the date 1494 on the bishop's bench end.
17	(Dean's stall): a demi-angel with a book or shield.
18	(Canon-in-Residence's stall): a lion attacked by dogs. (See Chapter 13 concerning the bench end).
19	A wyvern (a mythical two-winged dragon).
20	Angel with shield.
21	A wyvern with birds.
22	Hart's tongue ferns.
23	A very elaborate flower.
24	A lion attacking a monkey in a vine.
25	A vine with grapes.
26	Birds pecking fruit.
27	Two scimitar oryx (a type of antelope). The arm rests (not shown here) have ugly faces instead of the usual foliar patterns.
28	The first of three images which use a fox to parody a preacher. Here, the prior preaches to a gullible congregation (a duck and a hen).
29	Fox running off with geese (the Prior intends to misuse his flock).
30	Fox caught by dogs (justice for the congregation).
31	Mythical two-headed serpents fighting – these are known as *Amphisboena*.
32	A green man (fertility symbol), but carved upside down. There are other green men in the nave and at Fountains Abbey, at the north-east corner, carved just a few years earlier.
33	A hairy man (a wodehouse) holding a club, probably taken from the medieval tale of Orson and Valentine and the valorous slaying of giants in the woods.
34	(Mayor's stall): A griffin catches a rabbit while another rabbit disappears down a rabbit hole. The carving probably inspired 'Lewis Carroll' with his Alice stories. Chapter 13 commented upon the monkey (Photo 22, p.176).

APPENDIX 6

Figures on the pulpitum

The pulpitum is the massive stone screen which separates the Crossing from the Choir, supports the organ console and most of the organ pipes (see also Photo 26, p.180). The pulpit formerly stood on top of it, hence its name.

The figures, from left to right, are:-

1. Eadhed, possibly Bishop of Ripon from 681 - 686.

2. Willibrord: a Ripon-trained monk who was a missionary to the Low Countries and whose body rests today at Echternach, in Luxembourg. Note the Ward family shield, beneath.

3. Thurstan, Archbishop of York 1114 - 1141 who founded the Hospital of St Mary Magdalen in Ripon and also provided the land on which Fountains Abbey was built.

APPENDIX 6 (continued)

4. Matthew Hutton, Archbishop of York in 1604 when James I conferred collegiate status on the minster. The 'W' shield below is probably that of a 15th century wakeman.

5. King Athelstan. Chapter 1 gives details of his Liberty. Note the Pigott coat of arms below.

6. King Henry II.

7. King James I: see '4', above.

8. Charles Longley, first bishop of the revived See of Ripon in 1836.

APPENDIX 7

Choir Ceiling bosses

Many of the carved wooden bosses supporting the choir ceiling are medieval in origin, although they were re-inserted in the present wooden ceiling during Sir Gilbert Scott's renovation work.

Numbering from right to left (east to west), they depict:

1.   a head, which may represent God, the Father.

2.   probably showing the Good Samaritan helping an injured traveller.

3.   Adam and Eve being expelled from Paradise, at sword-point (Photo 23a, p.177).

4.   the Annunciation (Photo 23b, p.177).

5.   the Crucifixion (Photo 23c, p.177).

6.   a bishop and a king, enthroned, side-by-side (Photo 23d, p,177).

7.   a bishop giving a blessing.

8.   a king or Christ, enthroned, giving a blessing.

9.   a bishop, giving a blessing.

10.   a man leading a naked(?) woman to a church door (wedding ritual?).

11.   a head (Jesus?).

12.   an angel seated on a throne.

APPENDIX 8

Further reading suggestions

Most of the books listed below were used in writing this book. Some are available in the Ripon Public Library, mostly in the Reference section. More recent imprints of some may now be available.

Saxon Times

Bailey, R.N. *St Wilfrid Ripon and Hexham* in Karkov and Farrell (eds.) (1991), *Studies in Insular Art and Archaeology*, American Medieval Studies 1, (a critical examination of the structure of the crypts and of underlying concepts).

Colgrave, Bertram (tr., ed.) (1985), *The Life of Bishop Wilfrid by Eddius Stephanus*, Cambridge University Press.

Garmonsway, G.N. (ed.) (1978), *The Anglo-Saxon Chronicle:* J. M. Dent.

Lang, J. T. (1977), *Yorkshire Archaeological Journal, 49:* 63 (the Sigurd stone).

Shirley-Price, Leo (tr.) (1962), *Bede: A History of the English Church and People*, Penguin Books.

Taylor, H.M. and J. (1965), *Anglo-Saxon Architecture*, Cambridge University Press (details of the crypt, as established by the excavations of 1932).

Warin, Anne (1992), *Wilfrid*, York: William Sessions.

Ripon Cathedral (general)

Hall, R.A. (1995), *Antiquaries & Archaeology in and around Ripon Minster*, in Yorkshire Monasticism, Archaeology, Art & Architecture from the 7th to 16th Centuries (ed. Hoey, L.R.), British Archaeological Association Conference Transactions XVI.

Hallett, Cecil (1901), *Ripon: the Cathedral and See*, George Bell & Sons.

Parker, G. (c.1903), *Ripon Cathedral Church of St Peter and St Wilfrid*, Ripon: Kirkgate Press.

Smith, Lucius (1914), *The Story of Ripon Minster*, Leeds: Richard Jackson.

Walbran, J.R. (1976: reprint of 8th Edition, 1862), *A Guide to Ripon*, Easingwold: G.H. Smith.

Ripon Town and City

Anon (1892), *The Ripon Millenary Record.* Ripon: Wm. Harrison.

Ellis E., **Mauchline** M., **Pearson** E. and **Whitehead** J. (eds.) (1986), *A Ripon Record 1887-1986,* Chichester: Phillimore.

Fowler, Revd J.T. (Jan., 1896), The Account Book of William Wray, *The Antiquary,* Vol. 32, pp. 54-317 (several papers are relevant).

Ripon Minster and town in the Middle Ages

Anon (1882), The Ripon Poll Tax Return for 1379, *Yorkshire Archaeological Journal,* Vol. 7.

Burbridge, J. Paul (2008), *The Late Medieval Chantry Foundations and the Collegiate and Parish Church of Ripon*, Ripon: The Friends of Ripon Cathedral.

Surtees Society Publications, Durham (www.surteessociety.org.uk). Note: most of these texts are in Latin:

    (1874), II, Vol. 64, *The Ripon Chapter Acts*

    (1881), I, Vol. 74, *Memorials of Ripon Vol. I*

    (1884), I, Vol. 78, *Memorials of Ripon Vol. II*

    (1886), I, Vol. 81, *Memorials of Ripon Vol. III*. (This includes the *Paper Book*)

Werronnen, Stephen (2017), *Religion, Time and Memorial Culture in Late Medieval Ripon"*, Boydell Press, ISBN 978-0-86193-345-7.

Churches and craftsmen

Batsford, Harry and **Fry**, Charles (1943), *The Greater English Church, London:* B.T. Batsford Ltd.

Braun, Hugh (1972), *Cathedral Architecture,* London, Faber & Faber (written by an architect, an unusual and interesting book,).

Clark, Anne (1975), *Beasts and Bawdy,* London: J. M. Dent & Sons.

Crossley, F.H. (1947), *English Church Craftsmen,* London, B.T. Batsford Ltd.

Greenhill, F.A. (December, 1968), in *Transactions of the Monumental Brass Society*, Vol. X, part vi, pp. 461-464 (discusses the Ripon Lion).

Harvey, John (1975), *Medieval Craftsmanship,* London, B.T. Batsford Ltd.

Hudson, Kenneth (1978), *Exploring Cathedrals,* London: Teach Yourself Books.

Purvis, J.S. (1938), The Ripon School of Woodcarvers, in *Archaeologia*, Vol. 85, pp. 107-128.

Rowland, Beryl (1974), *Animals with Human Faces*, London: Allen & Unwin.

Sharp, Sir Cuthbert (ed.) (1840, reprinted 1975), *The Rising in the North: the 1569 Rebellion*, Durham: Shotton.

Surtees Society (1896) I Vol. 96 (gives details of Bromflets who were Freemen of the City of York).

Whellan, T. (1871), in *History and Topography of the City of York and North Riding*, Vol. 3 (mentions the alabaster carvings).

Archbishop Roger's church

Harrison, S. and **Barker**, P. Personal communication in the 1970s on the subject of *Archbishop Roger's Twelfth Century Church at Ripon*.

Miller, J. S. (1984-5), in *Annual Report of the Friends of Ripon Cathedral* (the Chapter House range of buildings is discussed).

Restorations

Anon, (1899), *Ripon Cathedral Past and Present*, Ripon: G. Parker.

There are also references in Hallett, Parker and the *Ripon Millenary Record*.

Gowland, Scott, Parker and **Walbran** (see below) discuss Blore's restoration.

Mortimer, Jean (ed.) (1951), Seventeenth century: Ripon Minster Fabric Accounts 1661-1676, in *Yorkshire Archaeol. Society Record Series* vol. cxviii – Miscellanea vi.

Scott, Sir G.G., (1874), Ripon Minster in *The Archaeological Journal, vol.* 31, pp. 309-318.

Nineteenth Century

Coleman, Terry (2000), in *The Railway Navvies*, London: Pimlico Publications (gives information about Elizabeth Garnett).

Gowland, T.S. (1943), The Minster and its Precincts, in *Yorkshire Archaeological Journal*, Vol. 35, pp. 271-287. (Gowland was a Ripon solicitor who spent much of his life compiling a history of the town and church and Yorkshire Archaeological Society holds his extensive collection of papers).

Other publications

see next page

The Cathedral Giftshop

offers books on varying aspects of the Cathedral, e.g.:

Beer, Malcolm S. and **Crawshaw**, Howard M. (2008), *Music at Ripon Cathedral 657-2008*, Chapter of Ripon Cathedral.

Clay, Nigel C. (2002) *The Gosney Statues*, Ripon: Ripon Jewel Press

Forsyth-Moser, Toria (ed.) (2010), *The Time Traveller's Treasure Chest – Josh and Tilly's Adventures in Ripon Cathedral*, Ripon Cathedral (a book for children).

Forsyth-Moser, Toria (ed.) (2008), *Who Do You think They Were? – The Memorials of Ripon Cathedral*, Ripon Cathedral.

Taylor, Maurice H. and **Ching**, Derek (2009), *Medieval Carvings of Ripon Cathedral*, Friends of Ripon Cathedral.

The Chapter of Ripon Cathedral (2018), *Glory in Glass, Windows in Ripon Cathedral*

Note on the Cathedral Library

Nearly all of the books belonging to the 'Cathedral Library', although still in the possession of the Dean and Chapter, Ripon Cathedral, are now housed in the Brotherton Library, University of Leeds.

Photo 1: the crypt as it is today

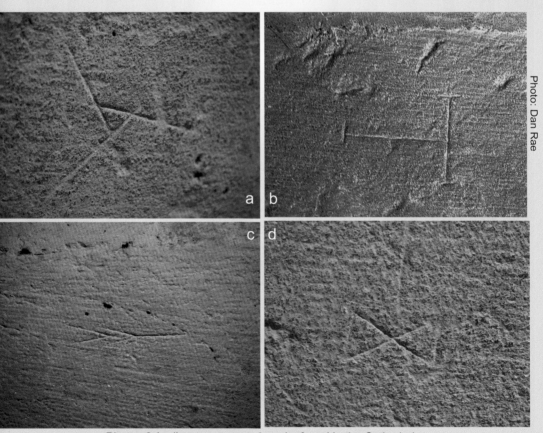

Photos 2 (a-d): some masons' marks found in the Cathedral

Photo: Dan Rae

Photo 3 - NW corner of Nave, above the Cathedral shop. The mismatch of stonework between the west facade and the earlier nave wall is clearly visible

Photo 4: Crack in Central tower wall (arrowed), and the massive rebuilt column below, are reminders of an earlier collapse in this area

Photo 5: in the SE corner of the North Transept, the uneven archway above the door has bee filled-in to stabilise the structure

Photo 6: after the partial collapse of the central tower in 1450, rebuilding commenced but was never completed as planned. The round arch is late Norman, but the pointed arch above the organ pipes much later

Photo 7: north end of the North Transept; for a short time, the stone masons used both (weak) round and (stronger) pointed arches

Above: Photo 10: Above the west end of the nave , apart from the present slated roof can be seen signs of other, earlier roof pitches

Photo 8: the three heads carved at this junction of an arch and a pillar in the choir cover a problem arising

Photo 9: a large buttress supporting the outer wall of the Chapter House

Below: Photo 12: The nave looking west. In addition to the two window tiers visible in the west end, there is a third rank of three windows in the roof-space; it can be seen from the outside (see photo on front cover)

NOTE: Photos 10 and 11, both by Bill Robson, appeared in the first edition of this book.

Photo 11: this massive pillar was built after the partial collapse of the centre tower, but its full load-bearing capacity was not used when the rebuilding work continued at higher levels.

600 years of stained and painted glass . . .

Above: Photo 14: the St Andrew medallion from the window (left), made from glass likely first made around the middle of the fourteenth century.

Below: Photo 15: a detail showing Saints Andrew and Peter from a modern window – the 'St Wilfrid' window by Harry Harvey, installed in 1977 (see Photo 38, p189)

Photo 13: the medallions in this nave window were assembled in the early 18th century from scraps of medieval stained glass

Photo 16 (a, b): two medieval alabaster carvings.

A third alabaster from the Cathedral, showing Christ's resurrection, is shown on the back cover

(a): St Wilfrid

(b): Coronation of the Virgin

Photo 17: The skill of stone carving is still required in restoration work today

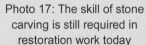

Photo: Bill Robson

Photo 18(a): fourteenth century sedilia (seats for priests) at the High Altar

Photo 18(b): a section of the hidden carvings under a sedilia canopy. These are visible only to a seated priest

Photo 19 (a): the better-preserved of the two Markenfied tombs in the Cathedral is actually the older, probably early fifteenth century. It shows Sir Thomas Markenfield and his wife

Photo 19(b): a closer view of the unusual neck collar shows a stag in a fenced field

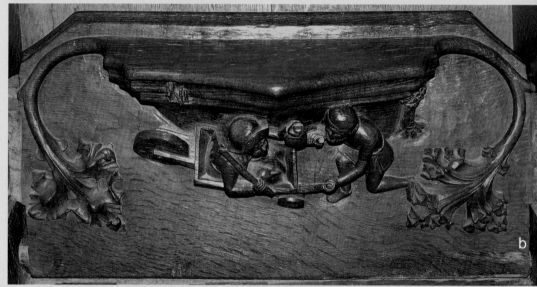

Above: Photos 20(a, b): two of Ripon Cathedral's fine medieval misericord carvings (see also Appendix 5).
(a) Joshua and Caleb carrying a large bunch of grapes, between two mythical part-human creatures
(b) Cuthman pushes his aged mother in a 3-wheeled barrow

Photo 21: the hand in the Choir, operated by the organist's foot, can be used as a conducting aid for the singers

Photo 22: an ape crowns the end of the choir stall reserved for the Mayor of Ripon

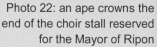

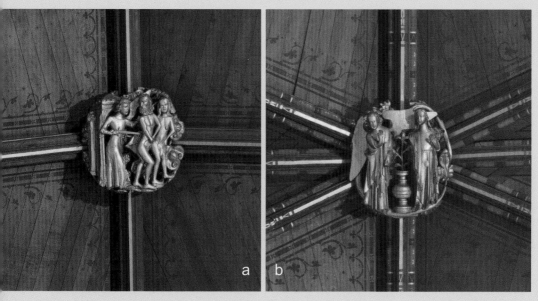

Photo 23 (a, b, c and d): four of the thirteen carved wooden bosses supporting the Choir ceiling:

(a) Adam and Eve being ejected from the Garden of Eden at sword-point

(b) the Annunciation of Christ by an Angel

(c) the Crucifixion

(d) throned figures of a bishop and a king

Photo 24 (above): detail of the finely carved medieval choir

Photo 25: (opposite page): the Choir stalls, canopies, organ loft, pipes and the fine ceiling, as seen from the High Altar

Photo 26: the pulpitum screen separates the Choir from the Crossing and Nave. The carved figures are named in Appendix 6

Photo 27: the stone font in St Peter's Chapel commemorates Bishop Moorman (1959-1976)

Photo 28: Niche in the South Transept: St Mary with Archbishops Roger and de Grey

Photo 29: a heavenly band – three of the twenty four angels in the upper level of the pulpitum screen

Photo 30: the oak staircase, screen and balcony donated in the late twentieth century leads to the Treasury (until recently, the Library)

Photo: Graham Hermon

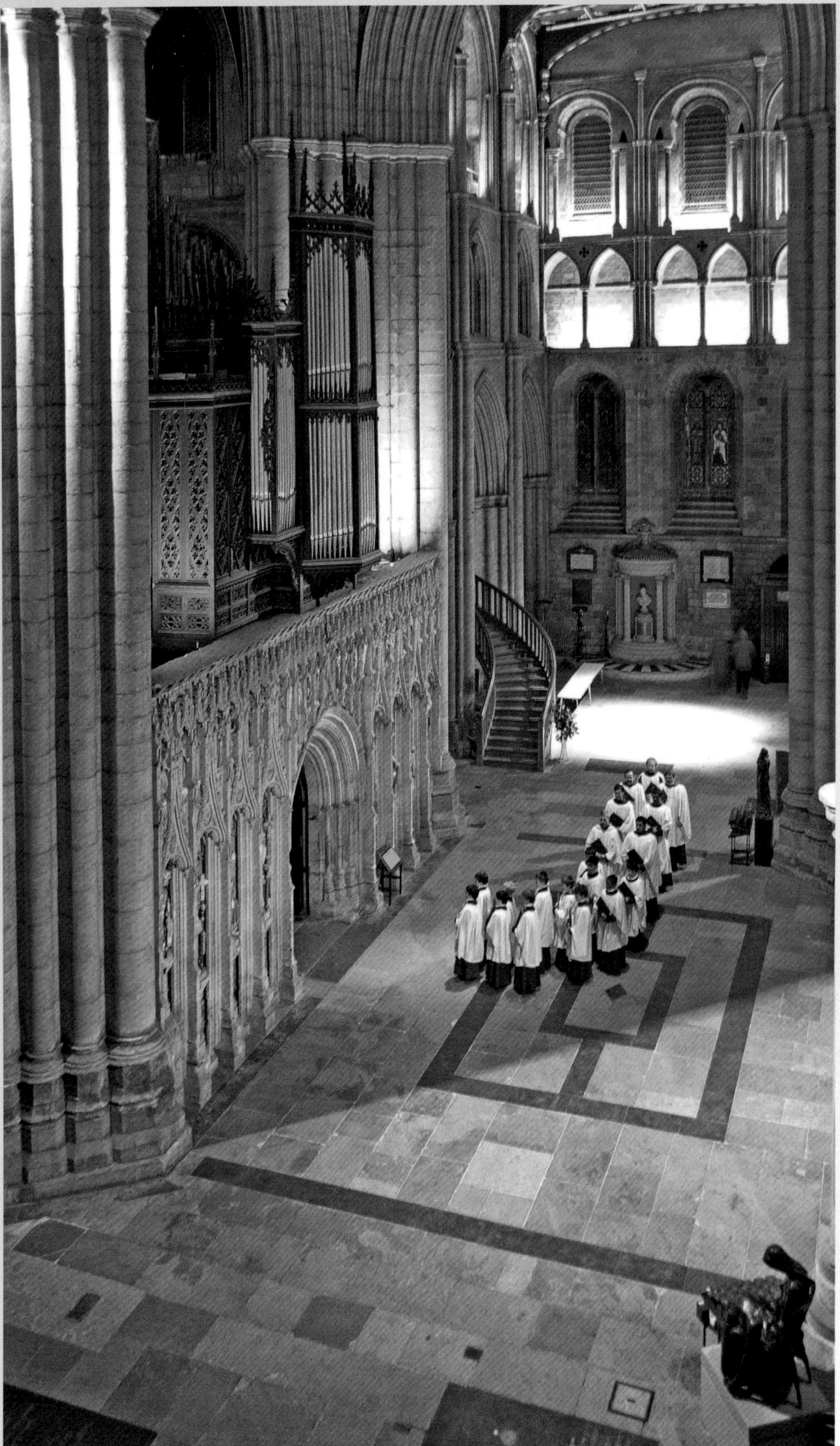

Photo: Graham Hermon

a

b

c

Photo 31
(opposite page):

The Crossing,
looking south.
The singers are
about to process
under the
Pulpitum arch
and into the choir
stalls

The Treasury
staircase and the
pieta statue can
also be seen

Photos 32 (a, b, c):

the triptych of
Harold Gosney
statues in copper:

Mary with Jesus as
a baby, a child and
after his crucifixion
(the pieta).

The sculptor
carried out the
work between
1998 and 2000.

Photo 33: the great East Window with the reredos below commemorating the dead of World War 1

Photo 35: St Hilda reputedly killed all the snakes at her Whity Abbey by throwing them over the cliff. This plaque on the 1913 pulpit is placed just above the sculpture of the Saint

Photo 34: the Arts and Crafts style pulpit installed in the Nave in 1913

Photo 36: this old stone pulpit now stands in the crossing. Its age has never been established

Photo 37: the twentieth century Reredos, designed by Sir Ninian Comper as a WW1 memorial

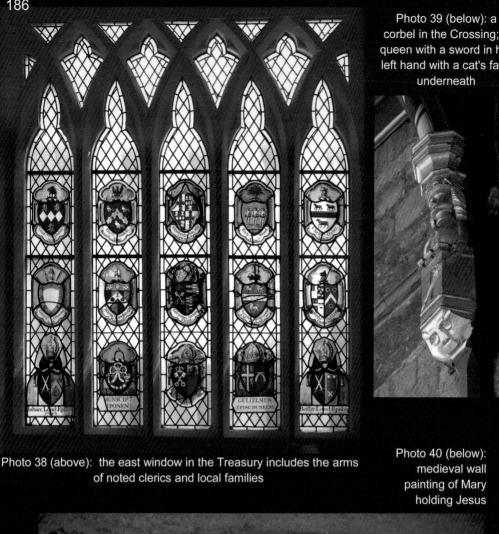

Photo 38 (above): the east window in the Treasury includes the arms of noted clerics and local families

Photo 40 (below): medieval wall painting of Mary holding Jesus

Photo 42: one of many fearsome-looking gargoyles

Photo 43: altar in the Chapel of Resurrection, made from an old 'drum stone', probably the base for an earlier column

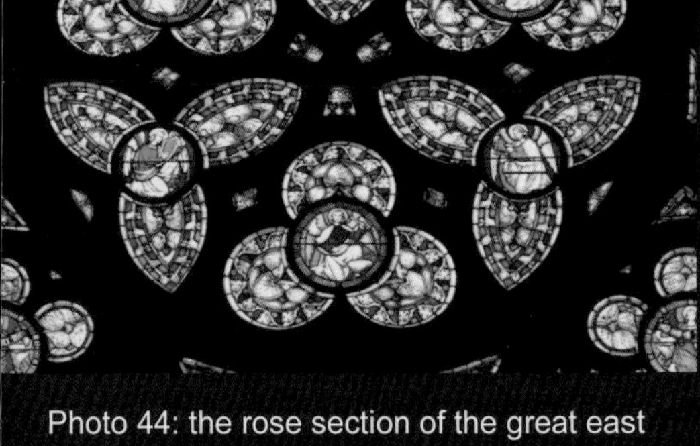

Photo 41: wood ceiling of the Nave

Photo 44: the rose section of the great east window of the Choir

Opposite top le

Photo 46: the 'Ru
and Naomi' windc
on the landir
outside the Treasu

Opposite bottom le

Photo 47: th
valuable work of th
Cathedral Flow
Guild is shown he
in the clev
matching of bloo
colours with the ne
cushion cover
which themselve
use the colours in th
'Christ' window abov
them (see photo c
le

Opposite righ

Photo 48: the 197
'St Wilfrid' window b
Harry Harve

Photo 45: the Chapel of Justice and Peace was established early in the twenty-first century. It incorporates the 2005 'Christ' window (John Lawson, Goddard & Gibbs) , the bishop's double canopy from the choir stalls, new oak altar table and chairs and new tapestry cushions on the medieval stone plinth

Editor's note: in 2014 the bishop's canopy was moved upwards to make space for a new 'Pity of War' panel, with words from Wilfred Owen's poems

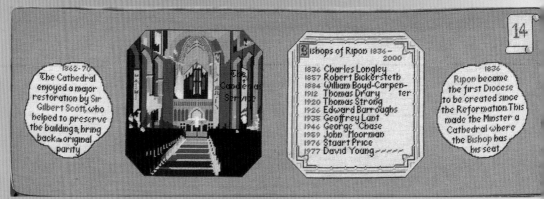

Photo 49 (above): one of 38 tapestry cushion covers made
by volunteers to mark the 2000 Millennium

Photo 50 (left): a corner
of the bell chamber in
the south-west tower
which now houses a
'ring' of 13 bells

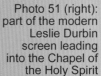

Photo 51 (right):
part of the modern
Leslie Durbin
screen leading
into the Chapel of
the Holy Spirit

Photo 52: aerial photo of Ripon Cathedral in 2009, as viewed from the south

Photo: P. Hills and D. Thelwall

Photos 53 (a, b, c):

three aspects of Ripon Cathedral at night in 2010 after installation
of new, low-energy floodlighting, the gift of a local benefactor.

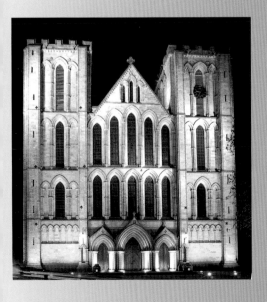

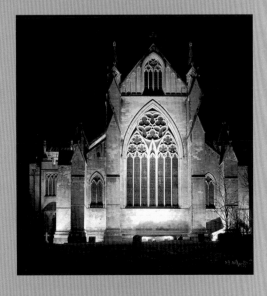

Index

Items highlighted in **bold** indicate illustrations.

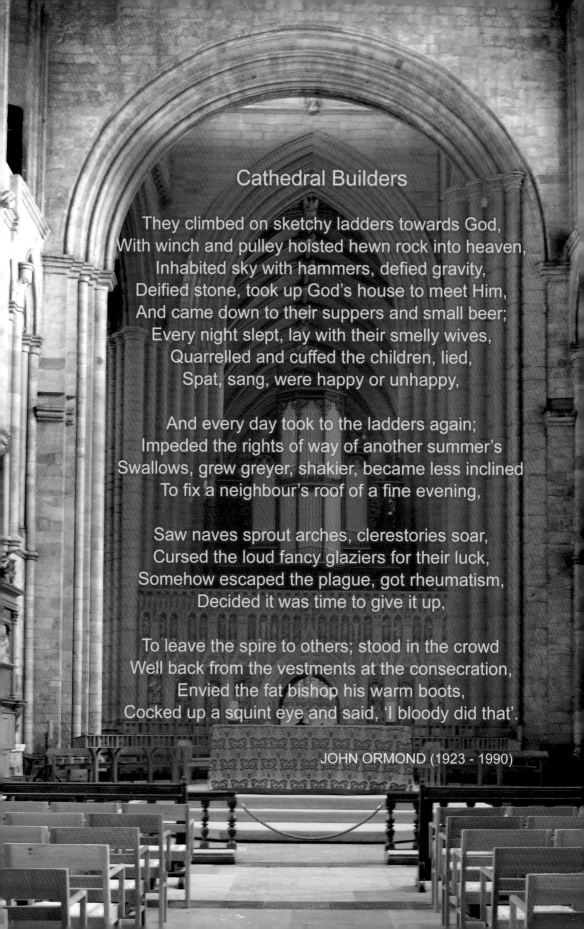

Cathedral Builders

They climbed on sketchy ladders towards God,
With winch and pulley hoisted hewn rock into heaven,
Inhabited sky with hammers, defied gravity,
Deified stone, took up God's house to meet Him,
And came down to their suppers and small beer;
Every night slept, lay with their smelly wives,
Quarrelled and cuffed the children, lied,
Spat, sang, were happy or unhappy,

And every day took to the ladders again;
Impeded the rights of way of another summer's
Swallows, grew greyer, shakier, became less inclined
To fix a neighbour's roof of a fine evening,

Saw naves sprout arches, clerestories soar,
Cursed the loud fancy glaziers for their luck,
Somehow escaped the plague, got rheumatism,
Decided it was time to give it up,

To leave the spire to others; stood in the crowd
Well back from the vestments at the consecration,
Envied the fat bishop his warm boots,
Cocked up a squint eye and said, 'I bloody did that'.

JOHN ORMOND (1923 - 1990)